MEDIUM AEVUM MONOGRAPHS

EDITORIAL COMMITTEE
K. P. CLARKE, A. J. LAPPIN, G. DAVIES
S. MOSSMAN, D. RUNDLE, P. RUSSELL, C. SAUNDERS

EDITOR FOR THIS VOLUME
A. J. LAPPIN

MEDIUM AEVUM MONOGRAPHS XLVIII

THOMAS HOCCLEVE'S TRILINGUAL GLOSSARY

A CRITICAL EDITION FROM LONDON, BRITISH LIBRARY, MANUSCRIPT HARLEY 219

EDITED BY
MISTY SCHIEBERLE

The Society for the Study of Medieval Languages and Literature
OXFORD MMXXV

THE SOCIETY FOR THE STUDY OF MEDIEVAL
LANGUAGES AND LITERATURE

OXFORD, 2025

http://aevum.space/monographs

© MISTY SCHIEBERLE

ISBN-13:

978-1-911694-27-4 (pb)
978-1-911694-28-1 (hb)
978-1-911694-29-8 (pdf)

British Library Cataloguing in Publication Data

A catalogue record for this book is available from the British Library

For Dee Ann

CONTENTS

Acknowledgements ix

Introduction xi

    Description of the manuscript xvi

    Audience xxi

    Description of Hoccleve's Glossary xxiv

    Hoccleve's French xxx

    Sources and Analogues in the Late Medieval Glossary
        Tradition xxxiii

    Hoccleve's Innovations in Structure and Recorded
        Language xl

    A Posited Connection between Hoccleve's Glossary and
        CUL MS Add. 8870 xlviii

    The Short Phrasebook in Harley 219 lii

    Editorial Principles lvi

    Abbreviations lviii

    Works Cited lix

Hoccleve's Trilingual Dictionary 1

Indices 81

    Index of All Words Used by Hoccleve 81

    Alphabetic List of French Words with Their Equivalents 101

    French Words without Translation 112

    Latin Words Used for Translation 113

Vernacular Words Used for Translation... 121
Index of Modern English Words Used as Glosses..................... 125
Dictionary Headwords Cited in the Notes to the Edition 137

ACKNOWLEDGMENTS

My work on London, British Library MS Harley 219 began out of a dogged interest in its unique version of Christine de Pizan's *Epistre Othea* and curiosity at the multilingual glossary, which we now know are both products of Thomas Hoccleve's hand. In preparing this edition, I have incurred many debts to colleagues and friends who were willing to spend time with me puzzling over manuscript abbreviations, paleography, unusual orthographic choices and enigmatic glosses. This project would neither have been possible nor nearly as rewarding (or fun) without their conversations and illuminating perspectives. My deepest gratitude always goes to Maura Nolan, Kathryn Kerby-Fulton, Jill Mann and Maureen Boulton, whose mentorship and friendship have been foundational to my study of manuscripts and the languages and literatures of medieval England; they have always supported my tugging on the strangest of threads and seeing what happens. I owe much of the advancement of my research to the unparalleled generosity of Anne Coldiron and David Wallace. R. D. Perry and Spencer Strub organized the New Chaucer Society panel that first gave me the opportunity to focus on the Harley 219 glossary and launched many fruitful conversations. Kerby-Fulton and Daniel Wakelin were early supporters of this editorial project, and I am grateful they shared their time, advice and resources with me. I am thoroughly indebted to colleagues who lent their expertise in Anglo-French and in medieval language learning texts: Jocelyn Wogan-Browne, Rory G. Critten, Thomas Hinton and J. R. Mattison, all generously spared time to review relevant sections of this project and offered guidance at critical stages. I also greatly benefitted from conver-sations with Christine Bourgeois, Kathy Krause, Sebastian Sobecki, David Watt and Sebastian Langdell. Their wisdom and advice helped me work through various linguistic, orthographic and paleo-graphic tangles across all three languages in the edition. John H. Baker kindly responded to my queries about the Cambridge manuscript, Ralph Hanna offered sug-gestions about provenance, and J. R. Mattison shared images and insights. I am grateful to the Medium Aevum Monograph Series editorial team for connecting me with a reviewer whose feedback was meticulous, encouraging and pleasant in offering advice and corrections. Anthony Lappin was instrumental in not only formatting the text and indices but also catching lingering errors. I have no doubt that infelicities remain, but my work has been strengthened by these colleagues' investments in this project and their incisive recommendations.

Closer to home, I wish to thank the University of Kansas, College of Liberal Arts and Sciences and the Department of English for supporting my editorial research and recognizing the value of this kind of scholarship. Much of my research would not be possible without the support of the KU Libraries Interlibrary Loan office, graciously headed by Nishon Hawkins, who seems to enjoy a scavenger hunt nearly as much as I do. Friends Jonathan Lamb, Darren Canady, Laura Mielke and Pritha Prasad generously allowed me to consult them over entertaining, earthy entries and challenging decisions, and they are always among my best sounding boards. Above all, I thank my family for their tolerance and support of my obsessions with medieval words in various languages, and especially my engineer husband, who is now complicit, since both our children have names of medieval French origin, which he not only allowed but encouraged. This project is dedicated to my mom, who first gifted me with a love for words, books and teaching.

INTRODUCTION

Thomas Hoccleve (*c.* 1367–1426) had a prolific career as a writer: for over forty years, he served as a clerk in the Royal Office of the Privy Seal, and for about twenty-five of those years, he was also engaged in writing original English poetry.[1] Hoccleve's compositions are notable for his remarkably modern portrayals of selfhood and anxieties in autobiographical poetry like the *Series*, for his political advice text *The Regiment of Princes*, for his translation of Christine de Pizan's *Epistre au dieu d'amours* into *The Epistle of Cupid*, and for his production of other short poems influenced by his bureaucratic occupation.[2] Often, elements

---

[1] For biography, see J. A. Burrow, *Thomas Hoccleve*, Authors of the Middle Ages 4 (Ashgate, 1994); Linne R. Mooney, 'Some New Light on Thomas Hoccleve', *SAC*, 29 (2007), pp. 293–340; Sheila Lindenbaum, 'Thomas Hoccleve', in *The Companion to Fifteenth-Century English Poetry*, ed. by Julia Boffey and A. S. G. Edwards (Boydell and Brewer, 2013), pp. 35–46; and Sebastian Sobecki, *Last Words: The Public Self and the Social Author in Late Medieval England* (Oxford University Press, 2020), pp. 65–100. Burrow estimates Hoccleve's birth year as most likely 1367, but Sobecki, *Last Words*, p. 83, has recently suggested 1368, based on his re-dating of the *Series*. Hoccleve was almost certainly born in London, since his father was active as a Draper there in 1365 and subsequent years; see Misty Schieberle, 'Thomas Hoccleve of London: New Evidence of Hoccleve's Family and Finances', *SAC*, 45 (2023), pp. 287–311. Hoccleve seems to have begun work at the Privy Seal in 1387 (see Burrow); Hoccleve dates *The Epistle of Cupid* to 1402 (his first known original production), and, as Sobecki, *Last Words*, persuasively argues, he produced literary texts up until very near the time of his death.

[2] On the interiority of Hoccleve's poetry, see Antony Hasler, 'Hoccleve's Unregimented Body', *Paragraph*, 13 (1990), pp. 164–83; Lee Patterson, '"What is Me?": Self and Society in the Poetry of Thomas Hoccleve', *SAC*, 23 (2001), pp. 437–70; and Sarah Tolmie, 'The Professional: Thomas Hoccleve', *SAC*, 29 (2007), pp. 341–73; on the *Series*, see David Watt, *The Making of Hoccleve's Series*, Exeter Medieval Texts Series (Liverpool University Press, 2013). For the petitionary and bureaucratic concepts that influence Hoccleve's poetry, see Ethan Knapp, *The Bureaucratic Muse: Thomas Hoccleve and the Literature of Late Medieval England* (Pennsylvania State University Press, 2001); and Robert J. Meyer-Lee, *Poets and Power from Chaucer to Wyatt* (Cambridge University Press, 2007), pp. 88–124.

of his poetry can be described as religious, moralizing or pastoral in nature, while shorter balades may be more playful and written for a circle of male friends and colleagues.[3] Many works show evidence of Hoccleve's frustrations at having trained for a religious clerical occupation within the Church but never being promoted to a benefice or position with stable income.[4]

---

[3] On Hoccleve's religious poetry (which includes Marian poetry, a screed against Lollardy and an *ars moriendi* treatise, some of which are translated and adapted from French or Latin sources) or moralizing or pastoral aspects to Hoccleve's poetry, see for example, Robyn Malo, 'Penitential Discourse in Hoccleve's *Series*', *SAC*, 34 (2012), pp. 277–305; Steven Rozenski, Jr., '"Your Ensaumple and Your Mirour": Hoccleve's Amplification of the Imagery and Intimacy of Henry Suso's *Ars Moriendi*', *Parergon*, 25 (2008), pp. 1–16; and Sebastian Langdell, *Thomas Hoccleve: Religious Reform, Transnational Poetics, and the Invention of Chaucer*, Exeter Medieval Texts Series (Liverpool University Press, 2018). On Hoccleve and masculine identity, see Holly Crocker, 'Engendering Affect in Hoccleve's Series', in *Medieval Affect, Feeling, and Emotion*, ed. by Crocker and Glenn D. Burger (Cambridge University Press, 2019), pp. 70–89; Isabel Davis, *Writing Masculinity in the Later Middle Ages* (Cambridge University Press, 2007), pp. 141–61; and Johnathan Stavsky, 'Hoccleve's Take on Chaucer and Christine de Pizan: Gender, Authorship, and Intertextuality in the "Epistre au dieu d'Amours", the "Letter of Cupid", and the "Series"', *Philological Quarterly*, 93 (2014), pp. 435–60. On patronage and audience, see Amy Vines, 'The Rehabilitation of Patronage in Hoccleve's Series', *Digital Philology*, 2 (2013), pp. 202–21; Rory G. Critten, *Author, Scribe, and Book in Late Medieval England, 1066–1550* (Brewer, 2018), pp. 57–58; and Sobecki, *Last Words*, especially pp. 77–78 and 95–100.

[4] The most commonly cited is his admission in the *Regiment of Princes*, ed. by Charles R. Blyth, Middle English Texts Series (Medieval Institute Press, 1999), ll. 1447–56, that he had hoped to be promoted to a benefice but finally resigned himself to marriage (and secular status). Knapp, *Bureaucratic Muse*, pp. 20–29, examines Hoccleve's autobiographical complaints and identification with a broad class of precariously-employed bureaucratic clerks. Kathryn Kerby-Fulton, *The Clerical Proletariat and the Resurgence of Medieval English Poetry* (University of Pennsylvania Press, 2021), insightfully places Hoccleve among other writers such as Langland and Audelay who confronted a crisis of unemployment or underemployment, in which worthy clerks were not promoted to church positions and suffered financial precarity as a result. Kerby-Fulton suggests that many of them supported (or attempted to support) themselves by writing or copying literary texts, which also served as an outlet for any pastoral sensibilities and for their frustrations.

Although hundreds of documents in Hoccleve's own handwriting exist from his work at the Royal Office of the Privy Seal, he also copied various literary texts and exemplars of administrative documents.⁵ There are much-studied holograph copies of his own English works in Durham, University Library, Manuscript Cosin V.III.9, and in San Marino, Henry E. Huntington Library, MSS HM 111 and HM 744; another Latin holograph manuscript was recently discovered in Cambridge, Trinity College MS O.7.43, which contains extracts from diplomatic and political letters, a chronology and personal notes.⁶ Hoccleve's hand occurs in short stints copying English poetry by John Gower and Geoffrey Chaucer in Cambridge, Trinity College, MS R.3.2 (the 'Trinity Gower'), and in Aberystwyth, National Library of Wales, Peniarth MS 392 D (the 'Hengwrt *Canterbury Tales*'), both large-scale productions of lengthy Middle English literary texts.⁷ Finally, Hoccleve's is the dominant hand in two multi-lingual productions: London, British Library, MSS Additional 24062, the 'Formulary' of sample letters Privy Seal clerks might be tasked with copying in French and Latin, and

---

5) For lists of MSS in Hoccleve's handwriting accepted by most scholars, see Burrow, *Thomas Hoccleve*, pp. 33–49; A. I. Doyle and M. B. Parkes, 'The Production of Copies of the *Canterbury Tales* and the *Confessio Amantis* in the Early Fifteenth Century', in *Scribes, Scripts, and Readers: Studies in the Communication, Presentation, and Dissemination of Medieval Texts*, ed. by M. B. Parkes, (Hambledon Press, 1991), pp. 201–48 (p. 220–23); Mooney, 'Some New Light', pp. 322–40; and Helen Killick, 'Thomas Hoccleve as Poet and Clerk' (unpublished doctoral thesis, University of York, 2010). For recent additions, see Misty Schieberle, 'A New Hoccleve Literary Manuscript: The Trilingual Miscellany in London, British Library, MS Harley 219', *RES*, 70 (2019), pp. 799–822, and Sebastian Sobecki, 'Gens sans argent: A New Holograph Manuscript by Thomas Hoccleve', *The Library*, 7th series, 25 (2024), pp. 121–46.

6) On Hoccleve's hand in the three holographs of his own works, see H. C. Schulz, 'Thomas Hoccleve, Scribe', *Speculum*, 12 (1937), pp. 71–81. For Trinity College MS O.7.43, see Sobecki, 'Gens sans argent'.

7) See Doyle and Parkes, 'The Production of Copies'. Simon Horobin, 'Thomas Hoccleve: Chaucer's First Editor?', *Chaucer Review*, 50 (2015), pp. 228–50, speculates that Hoccleve may have supervised copies of *The Canterbury Tales*, but for doubts see Lawrence Warner, *Chaucer's Scribes: London Textual Production, 1384–1432* (Cambridge University Press, 2018), pp. 115–33.

Harley 219, where he copies and collects literary texts in Latin and French that are followed by a trilingual glossary.⁸ Harley 219 thus offers a rare glimpse into Hoccleve's handwriting in all three languages in one volume, and in the case of the glossary, one single text, which he very likely compiled himself from existing available sources.

The text I refer to as 'Hoccleve's glossary' is more accurately a series of glossaries followed by a handful of short phrases, all copied into a jam-packed four folios of Harley 219 (147ᵛ–151ᵛ). Although most of the text is a list of French words and their definitions, Hoccleve compiles, adapts and rearranges content. He includes different parts of speech, conjugates various verbs (especially irregular ones), uses possessive pronouns for parts of the body and instructs the reader in different uses of the multi-purpose verb *faire*. But the subject-matter in Harley 219 is arguably unfocused and eclectic, as will be seen.

There is a long tradition in England of glossaries and texts for the instruction and reinforcement of French language skills that contextualize Hoccleve's production. The earliest surviving text promoting French language learning is Walter of Bibbesworth's thirteenth-century *Tretiz de langage* (1240–1250), a poetic text that focuses on preparing its pupil for household management by emphasizing terms for clothing, planting, breadmaking, household work, field workers, parts of a cart, decorating a home, preparing for a feast and so on. The *Tretiz* was frequently glossed, and eventually, glosses were extracted into vocabulary lists like the fifteenth-century *Femina nova*, which explicitly draws on Bibbesworth but fits more with the language instruction of Oxford schoolrooms, attempting to train future educated Englishmen for success in a trilingual society.⁹ To a certain extent, Hoccleve's glossary, which does show

---

8) On BL, MS Add. 24062, see Schulz, 'Thomas Hoccleve, Scribe', pp. 267–8. On MS Harley 219, see Schieberle, 'A New Hoccleve Literary Manuscript'.

9) For more on individualized glossed manuscripts of the *Tretiz*, see Philip Knox, 'The English Glosses in William of Bibbesworth's *Tretiz*', *Notes and Queries*, 60 (2013), 49–59, and Thomas Hinton, et al., *Learning French in Medieval England: The Manuscripts of Walter de Bibbesworth's 'Tretiz'*, an ongoing study at the University of Exeter, https://tretiz.exeter.ac.uk/ [accessed 30 July 2021]. For an introduction and edition of *Femina*, see William Rothwell (ed.), *Femina (Trinity College, Cambridge MS B.14.40)* (Anglo-Norman On-Line Hub, 2005), which explains the structure and practical purposes of the text on pp. i–iii. See

influence of *Tretiz*-inspirted vocabularies, might be classed with wordlists like *Femina*. Although Oxford is traditionally considered the center of language learning, there is some evidence of the transfer of Oxford French education and the students of Oxford language instructors (*dictatores*) to London.[10] Hoccleve's London pro-duction likewise suggests an interest in reinforcing knowledge of the French language among London and Westminster clerks.[11]

also Rothwell, 'The Place of *Femina* in Anglo-Norman Studies', *Studia Neophilologica*, 70 (1998), pp. 55–82; and Rothwell, 'Anglo-French and Middle English Vocabulary in "Femina Nova"', *Medium Aevum*, 69 (2000), pp. 34–58. As a caveat: previous scholars note orthographic 'errors' in *Femina*, while more recent commentators empahsize the variance that could be accommodated by medieval French; see, for example Claude Buridant, *Grammaire du français médiéval* (Éditions de linguistique et de philologie, 2019).

[10] One of the most famous *dictatores* was Thomas Sampson (fl. 1350–1409), who seems to have set up a sort of business school that could prepare students for administrative positions at home or perhaps abroad, consisting of instruction in letter-writing, in French language and in the drafting of basic legal and business documents. See H. G. Richardson, 'Business Training in Medieval Oxford', *American Historical Review*, 46 (1941), pp. 259–80; Nicholas Orme, *English Schools in the Middle Ages* (Methuen, 1973), pp. 75–8; and, especially relevant to the present conversation about London interest, Rory G. Critten, 'Practising French Conversation in Fifteenth-Century England', *MLR*, 110 (2015), pp. 927–45; 'French Didactics in Late Medieval and Early Modern England: Thinking Historically about Method', in *The History of Language Learning and Teaching: 16th-18th Century Europe*, ed. Nicola McLelland and Richard Smith (Legenda, 2018), pp. 33–51; and *French Lessons in Late-Medieval England: The Liber donati and Commune parlance* (Arc Humanities Press, 2023), pp. 6–9.

[11] On late medieval French learning materials as useful for reference and reinforcement, see Critten, *French Lessons*, pp. 12–13. On the status of French in England more broadly, see, for instance, *Language and Culture in Medieval Britain*, ed. Jocelyn Wogan-Browne, and others; Ardis Butterfield, *The Familiar Enemy: Chaucer, Language, and Nation in the Hundred Years War* (Oxford University Press, 2009); and the recent, sweeping study of hundreds of manuscripts containing French in England, J. R. Mattison, 'C'est livre est a moy: French Books and Fifteenth-Century England' (unpublished doctoral thesis, University of Toronto, 2021). On the multilingual contexts for clerks in the central government, see Gwilym Dodd, 'Trilingualism in the Medieval English Bureaucracy: The Use – and Disuse – of Languages in the Fifteenth-Century Privy Seal Office', *Journal of British Studies*, 51 (2012), pp. 253–83; and Laura

Yet Hoccleve's glossary is not a technical manual for clerical terms or administrative content relevant to his bureaucratic occupation. It much more resembles a general reference work that includes words for fear, dancing, doubt, mockery, jokes, rewards, reproach, anger, injury, bragging, causing trouble, cackling, tickling and much more, including language instruction and perhaps invention. As the final composition in Harley 219 that can be connected to Hoccleve, the glossary demonstrates a searching engagement with language and, added plausibly in the hand of a colleague, at least one explicit nod to Hoccleve's original poetry. If works like the *Tretiz* are motivated by a love of language and literary purposes as well as pedagogic instruction,[12] then Hoccleve's glossary may be seen within that broader lineage and within the growing interest in language texts among those living and working in London.

Description of the Manuscript

The majority of the Harley 219 trilingual miscellany was produced with Hoccleve not only copying various texts but also serving in a supervisory and correcting role.[13] Sebastian Sobecki's meticulous paleographical analysis demonstrates that the other five hands in the manuscript belong to scribes who worked with Hoccleve at the Privy Seal Office.[14] Sobecki persuasively proposes that the main contents were completed *c*. 1420, just prior to Hoccleve's composition of the *Series*.[15] But other elements

---

Wright, 'On variation in medieval mixed-language business writing', in *Code-Switching in Early English*, ed. by Herbert Schendl and Wright (De Gruyter, 2011), pp. 192–215.

[12] As Thomas Hinton has argued in 'Anglo-French in the Thirteenth Century: A Reappraisal of Walter of Bibbesworth's *Tretiz*', *MLR*, 112 (2017), 855–81, and 'Language, Morality, and Wordplay in Thirteenth-Century Anglo-French: The Poetry of Walter de Bibbesworth', *New Medieval Literatures*, 19 (2019), 89–120.

[13] For details of Hoccleve's hand, see Schieberle, 'A New Hoccleve Literary Manuscript', pp. 802–12.

[14] See Sebastian Sobecki, 'The Handwriting of Fifteenth-Century Privy Seal and Council Clerks', *RES*, 72 (2021), pp. 1–27.

[15] Sobecki, 'Handwriting', p. 12, refines the date based on Hoccleve's handwriting style, on the date of the *Series*, and on the date that John Offord, one of the scribes active in the copying Harley 219, departed for France (February 1420).

were likely copied earlier, like Christine de Pizan's *Epistre Othea*, which I suspect was copied near the time Christine sent poetry to Henry IV (*c.* 1401) and around the time that Hoccleve translated her *Epistre au dieu d'Amours* (1399) into *The Epistle of Cupid* (1402).[16]

The relatively small parchment codex (about 240 mm x 170 mm) shows evidence of use in wear, corrections and annotations throughout most of the volume. There are 154 numbered folios, primarily in quires of eight, usually with catchwords, and there are three codicological booklets: fols 1^r–79^v, fols 80^r–105^v, and fols 106^r–153^v.[17] The manuscript is remarkable for several reasons, perhaps first and foremost because it demonstrates Hoccleve and Privy Seal clerks copying literary texts, many of which are sources for Hoccleve's literary output.[18] The contents of the manuscript that can be associated with Hoccleve and his colleagues are as follows:

1. fols 1^r–37^r. Odo of Cheriton's Latin *Fables*: 66 fables, with what appear to be 49 original tales and moralizations not included in earlier manuscripts; some folios copied by Hoccleve, with assistance from another Privy Seal clerk.[19]

2. fols 37^r–79^v. *Gesta Romanorum*, Latin: 15 chapters (11 chapters from fols 37^r–71^r; fol. 71^v left blank; four chapters from fols 72^r–79^v);

---

[16] See Schieberle, 'A New Hoccleve Literary Manuscript', pp. 813–14. On Christine's connection to English aristocrats, see J. C. Laidlaw, 'Christine de Pizan, the Earl of Salisbury and Henry IV', *French Studies*, 36 (2), pp. 129–43. See also *Christine de Pizan: Epistre Othea*, ed. Gabriella Parussa (Geneva: Droz, 1999), p. 98 (hereafter, *Epistre Othea*).

[17] On fol. 153^v, two English prayers have been added in a sixteenth-century hand; on the flyleaf identified as fol. 154^r, a late fifteenth-century hand has copied a Latin recipe for the preservation of eyesight.

[18] Langdell, *Thomas Hoccleve*, pp. 59–60n58, points out these striking connections.

[19] Sobecki, 'Handwriting', p. 11, proposes Hoccleve's underclerk John Welde as a plausible assistant.

some folios copied by Hoccleve, with assistance from two other Privy Seal clerks.[20]

3. fols 80[r]–105[v]: an incomplete French translation of the pseudo-Aristotelian *Secretum Secretorum* given the title *Le livre du gouvernement des roys et des princes*, with table of contents, copied by John Offord, with some corrections by Hoccleve.[21]

4. fols 106[r]–147[r]: Christine de Pizan's *Epistre Othea* (the only complete *Othea* manuscript with dedication to Henry IV of England), copied by Hoccleve.[22]

5. fols 147[v]–151[v]: A glossary of French terms translated into Latin and/or Middle English, primarily copied by Hoccleve, with later additions perhaps by Hoccleve but more likely by Richard Priour.[23]

6. fols 152[v]–153[r]: 'Les offices accustumez destre donez par le tresorer dengleterre pur le temps esteant', a French list of officers employed by

---

[20] Sobecki, 'Handwriting', p. 11, notes similarities of the hands to those of John Hethe and Robert Frye. See also Sobecki, 'Authorized Realities: *The Gesta Romanorum* and Thomas Hoccleve's Poetics of Autobiography', *Speculum*, 98 (2023), pp. 536–58, for the importance of this manuscript evidence.

[21] Sobecki, 'Handwriting of Privy Seal Clerks', p. 7–11, describes Offord's hand, based on other documents, and identifies him as the scribe of the *Secretum Secretorum*. On Hoccleve's corrections, see Schieberle, 'A New Hoccleve Literary Manuscript', p. 812.

[22] Schieberle, 'A New Hoccleve Literary Manuscript', pp. 813–14. Stockholm, Kungliga Biblioteket, MS Vu 22, also contains the dedication to Henry, but it preserves only the short verse portions of the *Othea*. My assessment is that the Stockholm manuscript does not have any direct affiliation with Harley 219.

[23] Stephanie Downes, 'A "Frenche booke called the Pistill of Othea": Christine de Pizan's French in England', in *Language and Culture in Medieval Britain: The French of England c. 1100–1500*, ed. Jocelyn Wogan Browne and others (York Medieval Press, 2009), pp. 759–80, and Sobecki, 'Handwriting', p. 12, identify the hand of the additional lines as different from the main scribe (Hoccleve). The hand resembles Hoccleve's, as I noted in 'A New Hoccleve Literary Manuscript', but I am persuaded by Sobecki's detailed paleographical analysis of Priour's handwriting that he is likely a stronger candidate.

the Crown, added in a hand that can be attributed to the next generation of Privy Seal clerks, active in the 1440s and beyond.[24]

Harley 219 and its contents reveal significant information about Hoccleve's sources and literary output. As Sobecki has shown, the Harley 219 *Gesta Romanorum* texts are unique versions that Hoccleve used to translate the *Tale of Jereslaus' Wife* and *Tale of Jonathas*, and their textual evidence supports Hoccleve's claim in the *Series* that his original manuscript lacked the moralization for *Jereslaus' Wife*.[25] The *Epistre Othea* in Hoccleve's own hand confirms that he knew Christine's mirror for princes (and explains how the dedication to Henry IV came to be preserved in this rather average manuscript). The *Secretum Secretorum* demonstrates the likelihood that Hoccleve consulted this particular French version (after all, there were three French translations in circulation, in addition to Latin copies) to support work on his *Regiment of Princes*.[26] Less strongly connected to Hoccleve's English output, the Harley 219 copy of Odo's *Fables* provides 49 original tales and moralizations unattested in other manuscripts that may yet be linked with Hoccleve and his milieu.[27] Finally, and the chief topic of interest here, the trilingual glossary gives evidence not only of language learning in the early

---

[24] Sobecki, 'Handwriting', p. 11.

[25] Sobecki, 'Authorized Realities', demonstrates that the Harley 219 *Gesta Romanorum* tales are the sources for Hoccleve's *Series* translations and are the result of Hoccleve's alterations to the Latin texts, which rely on portions of varying manuscripts, including using one manuscript for the narrative of *Jereslaus' Wife* and another for its moralization.

[26] Schieberle, 'A New Hoccleve Literary Manuscript', pp. 813–19. On this unique French translation of the *Secretum Secretorum* and its other manuscript witnesses, see *Le Secret des Secrets: traduction du XVe siècle*, ed. by Denis Lorée (Champion, 2017). For sustained analysis of Hoccleve's *Regiment*, see Nicholas Perkins, *Hoccleve's Regiment of Princes: Counsel and Constraint* (Brewer, 2001).

[27] J. A. Herbert, *Catalogue of Romances in the British Museum* (British Museum, 1910), 3.50, identifies the additions, and they are printed in in Léopold Hervieux (ed.), *Les Fabulistes latins depuis le siècle d'Auguste jusqu'à la fin du moyen âge* (Firmin-Didot, 1896), 4.361–404. I am not aware of any posited source for these additions or whether they presently can be connected to Hoccleve's circle.

fifteenth century but also of how Hoccleve compiles, reorganizes and adds to existing wordlists, effectively creating a new glossary text.

Decoration in the manuscript is minimal and typical of most English manuscripts of this era. In fols 1ʳ–79ᵛ (*Fables* and *Gesta*) and fols 106ʳ–153ᵛ (*Epistre Othea*), there are blue initials decorated in red with fine red pen flourishes, red rubrication and blue or red pilcrows. The fols 80ʳ–105ᵛ (*Secretum Secretorum*) are stylistically distinct from the others, with black ink headings and black initials decorated with black pen flourishes; these folios feature more ornate ascenders and descenders on the first and last lines of text. The glossary shows no decorative features, only brackets that connect similar headwords or indicate when a headword and its gloss extend over more than one line.

Little is known about the manuscript's provenance until the seventeenth century. There are pen trials in fifteenth-century hands on fols 153ʳ⁻ᵛ, including a note 'Jhon Danger owe unto Thomas Barso' with pen trials and strokes around it that may indicate a sum of money; the name of John Bartolet; an English note containing the name John Gregori; the name John Jugo; and the relatively common Latin phrase 'dum sumus in mundo vivamus corde jocundo' [while we are in this world, we should live with a happy heart]. On fol. 152ʳ, a doodle of a face appears alongside the name 'William Lyes of Hadlye' (presumably Hadleigh in south Suffolk), in a sixteenth-century hand. None of these men has been identified, but there are some promising leads. A John Yugo was elected escheator of Lincoln's Inn in 1482.[28] While I have not located William Lyes of Hadleigh, Ralph Hanna called my attention to Robert Lyes of Stoke-by-Nayland in Suffolk, which is six or seven miles from Hadleigh, and who appears persistently in legal records of the third

---

[28] *Records of the Honorable Society of Lincoln's Inn: The Black Books*, vol. 1, from 1422–1586 (London, 1897), p. 76, https://archive.org/details/VOL114221586/page/n119/mode/2up?q=yugo [accessed 26 February 2024]. As Ralph Hanna informed me, there are also Prerogative Court of Canterbury wills that may indicate family members: Robert Jugo 'gentleman of London' (1501) and Robert Bartolet 'stockfishmonger of London' (1502) in London, The National Archives, PROB 11/12/245 and PROB 11/13/386 (personal communication, December 2023).

quarter of the sixteenth century and may have been a relative.[29] Both places are about 25 miles south of Stowlangtoft, the seat of the antiquarian Sir Simonds D'Ewes (1602–1650), whose library records indicate that the Harley 219 manuscript was in his possession in the seventeenth century; as Andrew Watson's classic study suggests, D'Ewes likely obtained some of his manuscripts locally.[30] In 1705, Sir Simonds D'Ewes's grandson sold the library to Robert Harley, the first Earl of Oxford and Mortimer (1661–1724), who collected and preserved an impressive number of medieval manuscripts. Harley's collection was sold to the nation in 1753 by his descendants and later became one of the foundational collections of the British Museum and then British Library.

Audience

Hoccleve's immediate audience most likely consisted of his colleagues in the Royal Office of the Privy Seal, not least because many of them helped produce the main texts in the manuscript, and others apparently added the manuscript's only practical professional text (the list of officers employed by the Crown) after Hoccleve's death. It might be tempting to see this glossary as designed to assist with the difficult French in the *Secretum Secretorum* or *Epistre Othea*, especially since it begins on the verso of the *Othea*'s final folio. However, the glossary is not organized as a reading aid, and any overlapping content with the manuscript's French texts seems at best a secondary consideration. The glossary records the dual meanings of *pois* (weight/pea) (fol. 149^r) and *amer* (to love/bitter) (fol. 149^v), which are essential to understanding central puns in Christine

---

[29] For example, London, The National Archives, Ward2/57B/205/77; Ward2/57B/205/78; Ward2/57B/209/1; Ward2/57B/209/2; Ward 2/57B/209/3. There is also a tutor of Oxford's Brasenose College named William Lye in 1562; see 'Appleyard-Azard', in *Alumni Oxonienses 1500-1714* (Oxford, 1891), pp. 29-50, available at *British History Online*, https://www.british-history.ac.uk/alumni-oxon/1500-1714/pp29-50 [accessed 4 April 2024]. Common names and multiple spelling variants make it difficult to identify the men, and Lyes in particular.

[30] Andrew Watson, *The Library of Sir Simonds D'Ewes* (British Museum, 1966). I am grateful to Ralph Hanna for suggesting the proximity of Hadleigh and Stoke-by-Nayland to Stowlangtoft as a path of possible acquisition for D'Ewes (personal communication, December 2023).

de Pizan's Chapters 2 and 13, but nothing points the casual reader toward this recognition.[31] The glossary also contains one of the few instances of *fumous* (noxious), a term only attested by the *Anglo-Norman Dictionary* (*AND*) in other manuscripts of this French translation of the *Secretum Secretorum* (fol. 149^v), but, again, nothing in the glossary acknowledges the word's appearance in the earlier literary text (fol. 98^v).[32] Nor does the glossary record the sort of French that would have been useful for civic or legal business (presumably professional jargon would be learned on the job, through formularies or treatises).[33] Instead, the glossary is more general, more interested in the workings of language and possibly encouraging experimentation with language.

Hoccleve and other clerks in the Royal Office of the Privy Seal functioned in a trilingual context. They were required to exhibit a high degree of competency in Latin and French, and they produced and processed documents that could include writs and responses written in English, French and Latin by various clerks during the administrative life and circulation of the documents.[34] Linguistic capabilities consti-tuted the professional identity for Hoccleve and his colleagues, and Gwilym Dodd has suggested that Hoccleve's *Formulary* – a collection of exemplars in French and Latin of the writs and letters frequently copied and processed by Privy Seal scribes – indicates Hoccleve's investment in government document production in French and in ensuring that his

---

[31] Chapter 2 of the *Othea* warns Hector of Troy that nothing would worth a pea if Temperance did not weigh things properly; chapter 13 establishes the goddess Minerva as Hector's metaphorical 'mere' (mother) and assures Hector that 'ne t'est amere' (she is not bitter toward you). Arguably terms like 'esbatre' (Harley 219, fol. 149^v) could also assist in translating Christine's multiple and sometimes overlapping usages regarding playing chess and appropriate forms of entertainment, but, again, the glossary offers no evidence of that intent. See *Epistre Othea*, pp. 203, 221, 317–18.

[32] AND, s.v., *fumous*.

[33] Compare to texts like *Femina* or the *Liber Donati* (Critten, *French Lessons*, pp. 37–38, 123–26), which seem more focused. See also Critten, 'French Didactics'.

[34] See Wright, 'On variation', and Dodd, 'Trilingualism'.

younger clerks had resources to brush up on their skills if needed.[35] If French were also regularly spoken in the office, as many scholars have proposed for government and legal offices, then the glossary could offer parallel support for participation in the daily life of the office, which may account for the conjugation of irregular verbs and some of the more jocular entries that could be fodder for amusement and office banter.[36] And, of course, although there is no evidence that Hoccleve traveled to France on official business, many of his colleagues did, including John Offord and John Hethe, the latter of whom produced high-end copies of treaties for the Duke of Burgundy and King of France.[37] The key point is that Hoccleve and his colleagues functioned in a multilingual environment, one in which a document like the trilingual glossary and multilingual texts in Harley 219 could be both edifying and enjoyable.

---

[35] See Dodd, 'Trilingualism', pp. 268–69; see also Philip Durkin, *Borrowed Words: A History of Loanwords in English* (Oxford University Press, 2014), pp. 229–35, who emphasizes that substantial linguistic competence in Anglo-French and Latin would have been required for anyone engaged in legal or governmental business up until the end of the fourteenth century, and Critten, *French Lessons*, p. 16, on language manuals as reference items. On Hoccleve's *Formulary*, which is London, British Library MS Additional 24062, see the edition by Elna-Jean Young Bentley, 'The Formulary of Thomas Hoccleve' (unpublished doctoral dissertation, Emory University, 1965); Watt, *Making of Thomas Hoccleve's 'Series'*, Chapter 4; and Matthew Clifton Brown, '"Lo, Heer the Fourme": Hoccleve's *Series*, *Formulary*, and Bureaucratic Textuality', *Exemplaria*, 23 (2011), pp. 27–49.

[36] On French as spoken language, see, for example, Butterfield, *Familiar Enemy*, pp. 31–23; W. M. Ormrod, 'The Use of English: Language, Law, and Political Culture in Fourteenth-Century England', *Speculum*, 78 (2003), pp. 750–87 (pp. 773–74); Lisa Jefferson, 'The Language and Vocabulary of the Fourteenth- and Fifteenth-Century Records of the Goldsmiths' Company', in *Multilingualism in Later Medieval Britain*, ed. by D. A. Trotter (Boydell and Brewer, 2000), pp. 175–211 (p. 184); Richard Ingham, 'Investigating Language Change Using Anglo-Norman Spoken and Written Register Data', *Linguistics*, 54 (2016), 381–410; and Rory G. Critten, 'The *Manières de Langage* as Evidence for the Use of Spoken French Within Fifteenth-Century England', *Forum for Modern Language Studies*, 55 (2018), 121–37.

[37] See Sobecki, 'Handwriting'.

Description of Hoccleve's Glossary

The fols 147ᵛ–151ᵛ that contain the glossary are divided into three columns of text, for which vertical and horizontal ruling lines remain visible; each column contains French headwords on the left generally followed by a Latin or French gloss. There is one exception to this format on the final fol. 151ᵛ, in which the left column is laid out in the same manner as previous folios, while the other two-thirds of the folio is a single, wider column that lists French words and phrases, with English translations to the right. Even though they use approximately the same amount of space for writing, fols 147ᵛ–151ʳ contain between 29–38 lines of text (the average is 32); spacing, size of letters and relationship of lines of text to ruling lines can be variable. The two columns on the final fol. 151ᵛ each have 24 lines of text, but the wider second column appears longer.

As I noted earlier, Hocclevc's glossary is more accurately a series of glossaries stitched together:

1. fols 147ᵛ–148ʳ. The first section lists terms, often grouped together, in a makeshift alphabetical order – in the sense that the first headword of groups in the first column begins with A, until groups with an initial headword beginning with B take over, and so on.

2. fols 148ʳ⁻ᵛ. In the final column of 148ʳ, *vener* and *vesser* are followed by *abatre* and other *–batre* terms, then a succession of entries that do not fit alphabetically or thematically; this brief 'section' of only thirteen headwords does not seem to fit into the alphabetical systems surrounding it.

3. fols 148ᵛ–149ᵛ. By the middle of fol. 148ᵛ, col. 1, a new loosely alphabetically-organized section begins; often subsequent words might appear or sound similar, e.g., *bras* (arms), *brais* (breeches) and *breis* (hot coals); or *gaigner* (to gain), *gainer* (to sheathe) and *guinher* (to wink). This section is one of the longest and extends from fol. 148ᵛ, col. 1, to the top of fol. 149ᵛ, col. 3.

4. fols 149ᵛ–150ʳ. The next section begins with the heading 'Hic secuntur verba equivoca' ('Here follow ambiguous words') on the last column of fol. 149ᵛ and extends to fol. 150ʳ, col. 1. There are 38 headwords that have dual meanings, followed by three phrases that illustrate idiomatic uses of the verb *faire*.

5. fol. 150^{r-v}. The rest of fol. 150^r, cols 2–3, lists names of the parts of the human body, followed by a companion list of the interior parts of the body on fol. 150^v, col. 1, with appropriate headings: 'Nomina membrorum humani corporis' ('Names of the members of the human body') and 'Interiora corporis' ('The interior of the body').

6. fol. 150^v–151^v. In col. 1, there is a space of two lines, then a list of clothing, a space of about four lines in col. 2, and a list of furniture, household items, various animals (domestic and wild), a few pieces of armor, various occupations and finally a hodgepodge mixture of plants, a couple of fish and six trees, which ends on fol. 151^v, col. 1. The spaces plausibly were left for headings that were not completed.

7. fol. 151^v. Finally, there is a makeshift phrasebook that runs across the other two-thirds of fol. 151^v, using the remaining space as one wide column, not two narrow ones.

Most of the glossary, from fol. 147^v through the first 13 lines of fol. 151^v, is in Hoccleve's hand, but on the final folio, there is a change of hand in the right column, at line 14, which seems likely to be the hand of Richard Priour, another Privy Seal clerk.[38] I have not found a full source in any extant nominales (wordlists) or phrasebooks, and at least some content is likely original to Hoccleve's compilation (see below on 'Sources and Analogues').

I am hesitant to offer tabulations and data on the glossary and its entries for multiple reasons. By my count, the total number of French words or phrases that are glossed is 782, but attempting to count the number of entries is fraught. Headwords are regularly jointed into sets of between 2–8 French terms that can be glossed by a single Latin or English term. If those groups count as one entry, then there would be 609 entries. Complicating matters further, there are often repetitions of headwords, e.g., *cheville, epar, cheure, scelle* and many other words appear twice across all the folios; *combatre* appears twice with different definitions with only one word between the two entries. Should each appearance count? In other instances, there are suggestions that Hoccleve (or his source) committed eyeskip between some headwords and glosses. For example, the mismatch between headword and gloss in *soiourer* –

---

[38] Sobecki, 'Handwriting', p. 12.

separare (to stay behind – to divide) and *signer – cingere* (to mark – to encircle) suggests that a scribe skipped from the headword to the gloss for a different term at least one line below in his source. Should an instance of suspected eyeskip be counted as one entry or as trace evidence of two? Rather than impose a view, I accept the uncertainty and focus on making the content available to other scholars who may wish to engage such thorny questions.

One might have an impulse to count how often English or Latin is used as the glossing language, but there are pitfalls to attempting to define a multilingual document in monolingual terms.[39] In a complex multilingual context, it can be challenging to establish whether a French term would have been recognized as foreign or as English, or whether the distinction would have mattered to the multilingual speaker or reader.[40] Considering those specifically trained for governmental and bureaucratic work, Durkin emphasizes the necessity of multilingual linguistic competence in English, Anglo-French and Latin through the end of the fourteenth century.[41] Some of these bureaucratic workers, including those in the Privy Seal, may well have used Latin to support their reading of French, but this is far from settled fact.[42] Many scholars once charted an overall decline in the linguistic proficiency of speakers of Anglo-French

---

[39] For a clear illustration of these challenges and pitfalls, see Wright, 'On variation', which illustrates how words in the context of a will might be read as English, Latin, French, English-French or even English-Latin, because the languages have so many points of correspondence.

[40] See David Trotter, '*Deinz certeins boundes*: Where does Anglo-Norman Begin and End?', *Romance Philology*, 67 (2013), 139–77; see also Tony Hunt, 'Code-Switching in Medical Texts', in *Multilingualism*, ed. Trotter, pp. 131–47 (pp. 131–32).

[41] Durkin, *Borrowed Words*, pp. 223–35. See also Hinton, 'Anglo-French in the Thirteenth Century', pp. 855–81, on the importance of clerks in the continued popularity of the *Tretiz*, and Ingham, 'Investigating Language Change', for legal contexts.

[42] See Christopher Cannon, 'Vernacular Latin', *Speculum*, 90 (2015), 641–53, and Thomas O'Donnell, 'The Gloss to Philippe de Thaon's Comput and the French of England's Beginnings', in *The French of Medieval England: Essays in Honour of Jocelyn Wogan-Browne*, ed. by Thelma Fenster and Carolyn P. Collette (Brewer, 2017), pp. 3–37. For concerns that the role of Latin in French learning is overstated, see Critten, *French Lessons*, pp. 16, 118–19.

after the Black Death and once English became more common as a language of official business from the late fourteenth century onwards, after such landmarks as the 1362 Statute of Pleading which specified that pleading in law courts ought to be in English rather than French.⁴³ Nevertheless, as recent research has shown, the Statute made little immediate impact, and any posited decline would occur much more slowly among widely read individuals whose professional identity was constituted by writing in multiple languages. As Richard Ingham has persuasively argued, Anglo-French was not a dying language, and late fourteenth-century clerks preserving Anglo-French in documents may have learned it as a second language yet still exhibited very high levels of proficiency.⁴⁴ Hoccleve, born *c.* 1367, was living and working in multilingual contexts across the very period when one might begin to trace the slow diminution of secondary language competency in Anglo-French.

The most I can confirm is that Latin is overwhelmingly preferred as the glossing language and that Hoccleve uses a mixture of Latin terms that are etymologically related to their French headword (e.g., *a travers/extransverso*, *ma langue/mea lingua*) and ones that are more abstruse. Of the glosses, only 176 are unambiguously English. Hoccleve's glossary does not follow the trend of identifying English words with *anglice* as other glossaries do, but he often records an article (*a* or *my*) or an infinitive form (often with *to*) to indicate an English gloss. However, he is not consistent in providing those pointers, and by my count, at least 25 entries may be Latin, but they could equally be recognized as English. These include a class of medical terms such as *pollex, labia, splen, cerebrum* and *medulla* that occur in the same form in Latin and English texts (see their MED entries); there are also ambiguous terms such as *mare, necesse, incantator* and *renes* that might be intended as Latin but

---

⁴³⁾ See the overview and important reassessment in Richard Ingham, 'The Maintenance of French in Later Medieval England', *Neuphilologische Mitteilungen*, 115 (2014), pp. 425–48; see also Durkin, *Borrowed Words*, pp. 231–33.

⁴⁴⁾ Ingham, 'Maintenance'; see also Richard Ingham, *The Transmission of Anglo-Norman: Language history and language acquisition* (John Benjamins Publishing, 2012), which shows that even when there is some evidence of declining native proficiency, high levels of second language proficiency were maintained during most of Hoccleve's lifetime. I am grateful to Jocelyn Wogan-Browne and Rory Critten for conversations about linguistic competencies and change.

might equally be received as English by fifteenth-century audiences.[45] In some instances, a gloss might belong to all three languages, e.g., *non* (which appears twice for a complex range of words: fol. 148ʳ, col. 3; fol. 149ʳ, col. 1).[46] There are also multilingual glosses. Most of the tree terms are glossed in both Latin and English; other glosses merge Latin and English (e.g., *Raye*, fol. 150ʳ; *scelle*, fol. 150ᵛ; and *vener, vesser*, fol. 148ʳ). The headword *aual* received two French glosses, *deius et parmy* (fol. 149ᵛ). Another entry arguably could be entirely French: *ades* glossed by *tost et continuelment* (fol. 149ᵛ).[47] Finally, there are 29 unglossed entries that leave a blank instead; among them, at least 19 French headwords are direct cognates to English. These cognates are most common in the sections on clothing and household items, e.g., *vne chemise, vne cote, vn doublet, vn bankeour, vne table*. For those entries, perhaps Hoccleve considered a definition unnecessary, but that rationale certainly does not apply to all the terms that are unglossed, e.g., *paleuole*, a term that also proved challenging for scholars to identify but which surely denotes a ladybird or a ladybug.[48] Moreover, on the final folio, one of the phrases is 'come len pooit dire cestui est villain rebours', translated as 'this is a froward cherl' – apparently the audience did not need the first half translated.

If, as seems likely, the initial audience consisted of Hoccleve's colleagues in the Royal Office of the Privy Seal, then the glossary's purpose may not have been language instruction but rather refining language use, and the sections on *faux amis* or false cognates might be

---

[45] MED, s.v., *necesse* has late attestations (1475–1500), though the first datable textual use is not always a certain indicator of a word's first linguistic occurrence; see Durkin, *Borrowed Words*, pp. 227–28.

[46] AND, s.v., *nun¹*; MED, s.v., *non* (adv. 1); DMLBS, s.v., *non*.

[47] The term *tost* might equally be a variant of Latin *tot*, but it is nevertheless a French word in its own right.

[48] Harley 219, fol. 151ʳ, col. 2. AND, s.v., *palevole*, expresses uncertainty about the varied definitions offered in medieval glossaries, as does Hope Emily Allen, '"Little King", "Sow", "Lady-Cow"', *The Journal of American Folklore*, 48 (1935), pp. 191–93 (p. 193). For Irish and Gascon equivalents that strongly indicate 'ladybird' as the solution, see Rita Caprini, '"Chenilles" et "coccinelles" en Gascogne', *Géolinguistique*, 19 (2019), https://journals.openedition.org/geolinguistique/1038 [accessed 22 December 2023].

particularly crucial for workers in a government office. Using a false cognate would immediately suggest a novice language learner, so reinforcing distinctions could be essential for workers whose professional status depended on their ability to compose fluidly in multiple languages. In many ways, the linguistic and historical circumstances in which new generations might be declining in proficiency in French makes the glossary a fitting companion to Hoccleve's *Formulary* as investments in supporting his junior successors' linguistic competence.[49]

In short, Hoccleve's working environment and audience were multilingual. By the fifteenth-century, Latin, Anglo-French and English have significant overlap and cannot always be differentiated as separate languages with precision or certainty.[50] It is challenging and perhaps even splitting hairs to impose modern assumptions about monolingual terms onto the rich multilingual environment in which Hoccleve operated – where French and Latin equally asserted influence on English writers and the languages they used.[51] What is fascinating about documents like Hoccleve's glossary, in my view, is that it embraces the three languages simultaneously and encourages reader facility in moving among them fluidly, rather than always insisting upon a strict delineation of languages.

Hoccleve's French

Differing sounds in English and the influence of English, and sometimes Scandinavian languages, are often responsible for spelling changes that are more commonly espoused in Anglo-French than Continental Fren-

---

[49] On the *Formulary*, see Dodd, 'Trilingualism', pp. 268–69.

[50] See Wright, 'On variation', especially pp. 206–07. See also Gwilym Dodd, 'The Spread of English in the Records of Central Government, 1400–1430', in *Vernacularity in England and Wales, c. 1300–1550*, ed. by Elisabeth Salter and Helen Wicker (Brepols, 2011), pp. 225–66, on the strong likelihood that early fifteenth-century clerks were allowed to write documents in whichever language they preferred, rather than being required by any official institutional policy to write in a particular language.

[51] Durkin, *Borrowed Words*, pp. 236–49, outlines the linguistic background in which English incorporated words from French, Latin, or both, and concludes that it is 'brutally reductive' to identify certain words as being of French or Latin origins when they contain the same roots (p. 247).

ches.⁵² Because of the fluidity of Hoccleve's multilingual environ-ment and the lack of 'standardized' spellings in the Middle Ages, I am reluctant to make sweeping claims about the orthography of the French in the glossary. Hoccleve relies on multiple source texts whose orthography may have influenced him in the moment of copying. There is also the likelihood that he might be influenced not only by Anglo-French forms but also by the range of forms circulating on the Continent.⁵³ Indeed, some of Hoccleve's forms or definitions are not found in the *Anglo-Norman Dictionary* (AND), but they are found in the *Dictionnaire du Moyen Français* (DMF), suggesting the currency and usage of forms not yet attested in the AND.⁵⁴ Still other meanings remain unattested.⁵⁵ And we know that Hoccleve had access to some texts whose originals were written in Parisian French, namely Christine de Pizan's *Epistre au dieu d'Amours* (which he translated into his *Epistle of Cupid*), her *Epistre Othea* (which he copied into Harley 219 himself), and perhaps the Harley 219 *Secretum Secretorum*, though the Harley 219

---

⁵²) See Ian Short, *Manual of Anglo-Norman*, 2nd ed. (Anglo-Norman Text Society, 2013), for characteristics of Anglo-French and Continental forms. I use 'Continental Frenches' to avoid giving preference to Parisian French, since other regions at various times might exert more influence or might exert simultaneous influence. For instance, Serge Lusignan, *Essai d'histoire sociolinguistique: le français picard au Moyen Âge* (Classiques Garnier, 2012), pp. 171–72, shows that Edward III's chancery used a Picard script for negotiations with Hainault, so one might expect to see Picard as well as Parisian influence in England, as one occasionally does (see further, pp. 167–85). See also David Trotter, 'Not as Eccentric as It Looks: Anglo-French and French French', *Forum for Modern Language Studies*, 39 (2003), 427-38. I thank Jocelyn Wogan-Browne and Rory Critten for discussions of these complexities.

⁵³) Hoccleve could have had access to literary manuscripts and government documents that might represent a variety of regional French forms. See Lusignan, *Essai d'histoire sociolinguistique*, pp. 171–72, on the influence of Picard in Edward III's chancery; and Trotter, 'Not as Eccentric'. Hoccleve's clerical colleagues who assisted in the production of Harley 219 also traveled to France, as Sobecki, 'Handwriting', pp. 5–7, 23–24, notes, where I assume they would have been influenced by forms and texts they encountered and may have brought back.

⁵⁴) Examples include *patiser* (fol. 147ᵛ), *marrir* (fol. 147ᵛ), *friande* (fol. 148ʳ).

⁵⁵) Examples include *compasser* (fol. 147ᵛ), *vener* (fol. 148ʳ).

copies are often inflected with Anglo-French by their English scribes.[56] On the whole, these variants in spelling and meaning invite us to recognize the flexible orthography and semantic breadth that could be accommodated by medieval French forms, far beyond those that tend to be recorded in printed dictionaries and modern reference works.

In general, the main orthographical features of Anglo-French include the following:

> *u* for *ou*, *o*
> *ei*, *e* for *oi*
> *aun*, *aust* for *an*, *ast*
> *k* for *qu* or *c*
> *w*, *gw* for *gu*
> *iw* for *iu*, *iv*[57]

The general reduction of diphthongs and levelling of vowels led to a great deal of orthographic variety in Anglo-French.[58] Vowels in hiatus could coalesce, or be split by the addition of *h*, *w*, *y* or *i*. In addition, weak *e* could disappear, or it might be added between *f*, *v*, *t*, *d* or *i* and a

---

[56] P. G. C. Campbell, 'Christine de Pisan en Angleterre', *Revue de littérature comparée*, 5 (1925), 659–70 (p. 664), list words whose Anglo-French spellings he takes to indicate that the scribe knew French poorly: *uncore* (for SMF *encore*), *taunt* (*tant*), *lesson* (*leçon*), *Joeudy* (*jeudi*). There is a strong likelihood that Hoccleve's source for Christine's *Epistre Othea* was the copy sent directly to Henry IV by Christine, either in her own hand or produced in her scriptorium; his source for her *Epistre au dieu d'Amours* may have been the same manuscript, or a copy she had sent to her friend and her son's warden, the Earl of Salisbury, that Henry IV had confiscated, as Laidlaw, 'Christine de Pizan, the Earl of Salisbury and Henry IV', proposes. A full study of the Harley 219 *Secretum Secretorum* has not been completed, but a quick review shows that it contains features common (though not necessarily exclusive) to Anglo-French, e.g., *uncore*, *Joenesse* (*jeunesse*), *seignur* (*seigneur*), *chivalers* (*chevaliers*). Presumably, Christine's manuscripts for Henry IV and the Earl would have been Parisian French, possibly in her own hand. The source manuscript for the Harley 219 *Secretum Secretorum* is unknown, and manuscripts vary widely; see Lorée, *Le Secret des Secrets*, pp. 23–45, 61–108.

[57] Short, *Manual*, includes an overview on pp. 45–46. See also W. W. Kibler, *An Introduction to Old French* (Modern Languages Association of America, 1984), pp. 203, 213–15, 225–26.

[58] Short, *Manual*, p. 45.

subsequent *r* (see Hoccleve's *fateras* for *fatras*).⁵⁹ Weak final *-e* as a gender-marker could also be lost. Certain consonants could be virtually interchangeable: *s, z, ss, sc, c* and *x* (e.g., Hoccleve's *fauxine* for *faussine*).⁶⁰ In Anglo-French the palatal *l* and *n* tended to depalatize, resulting in spellings like *seinur* for *seignur* and *esluiner* for *esluigner*. There could be generalization of *le* for *la* and *li*; confusion of *li* and *lui*; or alternate spellings for *je*. Consonants might be doubled; consonants dropped by Continental Frenches might reappear in Anglo-French (e.g., *espingles* for *épingle*). And it must be cautioned that not all of these traits occur consistently among all users of Anglo-French or occur exclusively in Anglo-French (e.g., generalization of *le* for *la* and *li* is also characteristic of Picard).⁶¹

Some of these traits are on display in Hoccleve's glossary: *fateras* for *fatras*, *faceoun* for *façon*, *launce* for *lance*, *Baroun* for *baron*; *paour* for *pour*; *makereu* and *makerelle* for *maquereau* and *maquerelle*. But the above-mentioned broad tendencies are not always evident, as his spellings include *monseigneur* and *gaigner*, and the phrasebook entries always use *Je*. Sometimes it may seem as though offering various French possibilities is the point: Hoccleve pairs *greignour* and *greindre*, which are variant forms of the same comparative adjective, and the visual spelling *gaigner* is crucial to differentiating this term and its meaning from the subsequent homophone *gainer*. If the AND entry is correct, Hoccleve's would be the first attestation of *gainer* (to sheathe) in an Anglo-French context.⁶² Thus this multilingual glossary may well yield useful additions to our understanding of Anglo-French terms in circulation and their spellings, but it is beyond the scope of this project to undertake a sustained study of all the orthographical complexities in the glossary and its neighboring

---

⁵⁹⁾ Short, *Manual*, p. 45.

⁶⁰⁾ Short, Manual, p. 46. See also E. Einhorn, *Old French: A Concise Handbook* (Cambridge University Press, 1974), pp. 140–41.

⁶¹⁾ For a concise account of the complexities of medieval French in Europe, across national boundaries and focused beyond Paris, see Jane Gilbert, Simon Gaunt and William Burgwinkle, *Medieval French Literary Culture Abroad* (Oxford University Press, 2020), pp. 1–20.

⁶²⁾ AND, s.v., *gainer, waynter*, and *gainer*; DMF, s.v., *graindre*; TL, s.v., *graignor*.

literary texts, which would be needed for a fuller sense of the practices of the Privy Seal clerks whose writing appears in Harley 219.

Sources and Analogues in the Late Medieval Glossary Tradition

Many scholars have offered histories of glossaries and dictionaries, so I will not repeat their work here, simply note that an Englishman had not produced a formalized, alphabetical French-to-English dictionary approaching what modern readers expect until Randle Cotgrave's *A Dictionarie of the French and English Tongues*, printed by Adam Islip in London in 1611.[63] Often the focus of study has been on glosses and wordlists that support the learning of Latin, with glosses in English and/or French. In the fourteenth and fifteenth centuries, there are many manuals and wordlists that focus on instruction in French language and vocabulary for English learners, some of which seem to expect that the student is already familiar enough with Latin that it can be used as a glossing language. As a result, scholars have disputed the degree to which such language learning aids demonstrate that French was falling into disuse as a native language. However, as noted above, strong cases have been made that French linguistic competence was maintained through the fourteenth century, and, moreover, that some manuals previously asserted as proof of French's decline were not aimed at beginners but

---

[63] *STC*, 2nd ed., 5830. John Palsgrave's *Lesclarcissement de la langue francoyse* (London, 1530; *STC*, 2nd ed., 19166) predates Cotgrave, but it is a more comprehensive manual of instruction in the French language, and its alphabetized lists prioritize English headwords, separated out by parts of speech (nouns, adjective, pronouns, verbs, etc.); French equivalent terms are then provided, often with synonyms and sample sentences. Cotgrave reprints and augments the Huguenot Claudius Hollyband's *The treasurie of the French tong* (London, 1580; *STC*, 2nd ed., 6761), a text later reprinted as *A dictionarie French and English* (London, 1593; *STC*, 2nd ed., 6737). On the history of dictionaries, see, for example, *The Oxford History of English Lexicography*, Vol. 1, ed. by A. P. Cowie (Oxford, 2009), especially the overview by Hans Sauer, 'Glosses, Glossaries, and Dictionaries in the Medieval Period', pp. 17–40; Tony Hunt, *Teaching and Learning Latin in Thirteenth-Century England*, 3 vols (Brewer, 1991); and the essays collected in *Ashgate Critical Essays on Early English Lexicographers, Volume 2: Middle English*, ed. by Christine Franzen (Ashgate, 2011). See also, on language education and model dialogues, Critten, *French Lessons*, pp. 1–24.

rather were intended as references and reinforcement for audiences already generally competent in French.[64]

Evidence for continued use of French in central government documents and the proliferation of French literary manuscripts purchased by Englishmen during the Hundred Years' War further suggests that the language and its literature were valued, and understood, by many, enough to warrant consideration of French and English as 'co-vernaculars', at least among certain sectors in society.[65] The translation projects that adapted Continental French texts to English audiences – Hoccleve's own *Epistle of Cupid* and 'Complaint Paramount', Stephen Scrope's *Epistle of Othea*, John Lydgate's translations of DeGuileville and Premierfait, among others, including many anonymous productions – do not necessarily mean that their audiences did not know French.[66] Those translations potentially enabled the authors to reach wider audiences but also, and perhaps more crucially, to demonstrate their own participation in an already-established Francophone and emergent Anglophone high literary culture. Of course, Hoccleve and his colleagues would have used French regularly in their bureaucratic day jobs. The content copied into Harley MS 219 suggests that they were also invested in literary texts, but I read the glossary not as directly facilitating their work or their leisurely enjoyment of specific literary texts. Rather, I see it as a more general reference work that could reinforce knowledge of language but also support experimentation with language, organization of content, and playfulness in the process.

Hoccleve's glossary draws on multiple resources for its content, and in the broadest of terms, it draws on the tradition initiated by Bibbes-

---

[64] See Ingham, 'Maintenance', and *Transmission*, and Critten, *French Lessons*, p. 16.

[65] See Butterfield, *Familiar Enemy*; on literary exchange and vernacular poetic projects, see Elizaveta Strakhov, *Continental England: Form, Translation, and Chaucer in the Hundred Years' War* (Ohio State University Press, 2022).

[66] For example, Hoccleve's *Epistle of Cupid* would have been unnecessary to his earliest audiences who would have been familiar with French: King Henry IV, courtly circles and his own clerical circles. Stephen Scrope's *Epistle of Othea* was produced from a French copy that his stepfather John Fastolf owned; as Sonja Drimmer, 'Failure before Print (The Case of Stephen Scrope)', *Viator*, 46 (2015), pp. 343–72, rightly points out, Fastolf may not have wanted, much less needed, the translation.

worth's thirteenth-century *Tretiz*.⁶⁷ The *Tretiz* is a popular and influential lyrical Anglo-French text designed to educate the rural aristocracy. Almost all extant *Tretiz* manuscripts contain glosses into Middle English (and glosses in each individual manuscript vary widely).⁶⁸ Some derivative texts are adapted for alternative audiences, like the fifteenth-century *Femina*, which appends to the *Tretiz* lyrics, proverbs and moral content aimed at preparing a more generally intellectual, clerical audience to be rhetorically wise in their speech.⁶⁹ More often in the fifteenth-century, the content of the *Tretiz* lyrics is distilled into vocabulary lists or *nominalia*, which present Anglo-French terms glossed into Latin or

---

⁶⁷) In addition to the *Tretiz*, other language-learning texts and wordlists existed, but I have not found similar content in the *Orthographia Gallica*, ed. R. C. Johnston, Plain Texts Series 5 (Anglo-Norman Text Society, 1987); *Liber Donati*, ed. Brian Merrilees and Beata Sitarz-Fitzpatrick, Plain Texts Series 9 (Anglo-Norman Text Society, 1993); Critten, *French Lessons*; or any of the series of conversations that traveled under the name *Manière de langage*, which may be consulted in Andres M. Kristol (ed.), *Manières de langage (1396, 1399, 1415)*, Anglo-Norman Texts 53 (Anglo-Norman Text Society, 1995). Furthermore, any overlapping content in *Femina*, in W. W. Skeat, ed., 'Nominale sive Verbale', *Transactions of the Philological Society* (1906), pp. 1*–50*, or in Tony Hunt, ed. 'The Trilingual Vocabulary in MS Westminster Abbey 34/11', *NQ*, 226 (1981), pp. 14–15, appears to derive from the fact that all share the *Tretiz* as an ancestor, not from direct relationships. On how texts like the *Manières* might have been used in England, see Critten, 'Practising'.

⁶⁸) For more on these individualized glossed *Tretiz* manuscripts, see Hinton, et al., *Learning French in Medieval England*, https://tretiz.exeter.ac.uk/ [accessed 30 July 2021], and Knox, 'The English Glosses'.

⁶⁹) For the lines that indicate that one goal of the text is to instruct the reader in using speech, and the French language in particularly, wisely, see Rothwell, ed., *Femina*, pp. 85–87. On the audience as members of an administrative class of clerks, see Rothwell, 'Anglo-French and Middle English Vocabulary in "Femina Nova"'; and Rothwell, ed., *Femina*, pp. i–iii. See also Hinton, 'Anglo-French in the Thirteenth Century', for the suggestion that even earlier, the *Tretiz* was popular among clerical audiences.

Middle English, and more rarely a mixture of both.[70] The proliferation of such resources demonstrates the consistent importance of French as a language of status, business, law and government communication during the late medieval period, regardless of whether it was a native or learned language.[71]

Medieval wordlists in the *Tretiz* tradition organize content thematically – not alphabetically – to provide a contextual basis for knowledge.[72] Latin headings often signal the major groups: parts of the body, rooms of a house and the items found in each, clothing, animals, birds, trees and so on. Within these groups, words are organized spatially, i.e., head to toe, around the room or in further organizational subgroups – exterior body parts then interior, domestic animals then wild animals. In extracting terms from Bibbesworth's lyrical composition, later *nominalia* may rearrange content. For example, Bibbesworth interweaves homonyms or near homonyms – words that might be misunderstood – wherever one appeared. Within the section on the human body, he pauses to clarify *la levere* (the lip) against *le levere* (the hare), *la livere* (the pound) and *le livre* (the book) and to differentiate between *kevil* (ankle) and *kyvil* (pin).[73] Later *nominalia* eschew placing hares, pounds and books within the subgroup devoted to the body: the fifteenth-century

---

[70] There are a variety of these *nominalia*, and generally they proceed either in Latin and Anglo-French or Anglo-French and Middle English. See, for example, the Anglo-French and Latin list in Tony Hunt, 'The Anglo-Norman Vocabularies in MS Oxford, Bodleian Library, Douce 88', *Medium Aevum*, 49 (1980), pp. 5–25; and the 'Nominale sive Verbale', which at times offers sentences, rather than just lists of words. See also Hunt, ed., 'The Trilingual Vocabulary in MS Westminster Abbey 34/11', for a *nominale* of French words with Latin and Middle English glosses.

[71] Ingham, *Transmission*, pp. 159–63, concludes that evidence of French as a learned second language only begins to show at the end of the fourteenth-century, and there are still high levels of proficiency among clerks. See also Dodd, 'Trilingualism'; Wright, 'On variation'; Ormrod, 'Use of English'.

[72] But see the fragment of a wordlist in the *Liber Donati*, which provides 43 French verb infinitives beginning with *a* and nine beginning with *b* in alphabetical order, in Critten, *French Lessons*, pp. 37–38, with commentary pp. 123–28.

[73] *Walter de Bibbesworth: Le Tretiz*, ed. by William Rothwell (Anglo-Norman Text Society), ll. 61–66, 151–56.

'Nominale sive Verbale' places this group of four terms instead with other easily confused words hundreds of lines later.[74]

Hoccleve's final sections on body parts, furniture, clothing, animals and trees ultimately have precedent in Bibbesworth's *Tretiz*, but it is not his direct source. Hoccleve appears to have accessed the material through an intermediary *nominale* that likely resembled the one in Cambridge University Library, MS Additional 8870, which has been dated to the first half of the fifteenth century (hereafter, CUL Add. 8870). Alongside various French legal texts and a French phrasebook, the Cambridge *nominale* occasionally provides English glosses instead of Latin ones, prefaced with *anglice* to indicate the shift in glossing language.[75] Because this wordlist and Hoccleve's glossary exhibit some shared atypical entries, I propose that they shared a source, and I use CUL Add. 8870 to inform my analysis of Harley 219.[76] For instance, among the body parts, Harley

---

[74] 'Nominale sive Verbale', ll. 626–33.

[75] Providing the marker *anglice* is not uncommon; Christopher Cannon, *From Literacy to Literature, England, 1300–1400* (Oxford University Press, 2016), pp. 28–29, observes that such Latin markers are repeated reminders to students of which vernacular language is used. See, for example, Hunt, *Teaching and Learning Latin*, ii, pp. 125–45, for *anglice* or *a.* marking English glosses to John of Garland's *Dictionarius*, sometimes complementing *gallice*.

[76] J. H. Baker, 'A French Vocabulary and Conversation-Guide in a Fifteenth-Century Legal Notebook', *Medium Aevum*, 58 (1989), 80–103, has analyzed this manuscript in detail; I am grateful to Baker (personal correspondence) for confirming that the notebook in question now carries the shelfmark CUL Add. MS 8870. As Baker, 'A French Vocabulary', pp. 81–82, observed, the CUL Add. MS 8870 *nominale* has at least two sections that are 'derived directly or indirectly' from Bibbesworth's *Tretiz*, and the list of body parts resembles the 'Nominale sive Verbale', which Skeat published from Cambridge University Library, MS Ee.iv.20. In my view, the 'Nominale sive Verbale' list has enough differences that it should not be considered a close analogue. To my knowledge, no other Anglo-Norman glossaries contain substantial content similar to CUL Add. 8870 and Harley 219: there may be occasional overlap, but shared entries seem typical of the genre and derivative from Bibbesworth's *Tretiz*. I have found no substantial overlap in Hoccleve's glossary with *Femina nova*; Kristol, *Manières de langage*; or other *nominalia* like 'Nominale sive Verbale' or the wordlist in Westminster MS 34/11. *Orthographia Gallica*, ed. Johnston, pp. 17–18, provides a general model of how one might organize language learning, but there is no discernible influence on Harley 219 or CUL Add. MS 8870. Any similarities are

219 and CUL Add. 8870 both include the genitalia (omitted from both Bibbesworth and *Femina*), both feature some unusual words, and both add the four humours after the body parts.[77] J. H. Baker notes that, compared to Bibbesworth, *Femina*, and 'Nominale sive Verbale', CUL Add. 8870 contains about eighty words not found in other *nominalia*.[78] Some of these terms are shared with Hoccleve's Harley 219 content (though others are in sections that Hoccleve omits). In other cases, words shared in other nominalia are glossed differently in CUL Add. 8870 and Harley 219, e.g., for fox, one finds *regnart* (in CUL Add. 8870 and Harley 219) instead of or in addition to *gopil* (in Bibbesworth, *Femina*, 'Nominale sive Verbale' and Harley 219); for weasel, one finds *fouvyn* or *mustole* instead of *beleth* (in Bibbesworth) or *welet* (in *Nominale sive Verbale*).[79] Baker also notes some new additions in CUL Add. 8870, such as *cotyhardy*, *jupon*, *mytens*, *mymonet*, *marmoset*; these are likewise found in Harley 219.[80] There are other similarities, too. Hoccleve and the Cambridge scribe group the same terms together as synonyms even when they are not exactly equivalent: *brinde* and *freint* are technically two different parts of a bridle, and a castrated ram should not be grouped

---

due not to influence or a shared direct source but rather to indirect sources (like the *Tretiz*) or commonplace mentalities or memories in the organization and production of language learning texts. Patrizia Lendinaria, 'The glossary in MS Cambridge, St. John's College, E.17 and Middle English lexicography', *Germanic Philology*, 7 (2015), pp. 89–140, examines a short French-English nominale with a similarly broad relationship to other *nominalia* of the later Middle Ages.

[77] Baker, 'A French Vocabulary', p. 82, notes that the 'Nominale sive Verbale' includes the genitals and four humours. However, the words listed are not quite the same and are in a different order. Among other differences in the body part section alone, the 'Nominale' glosses *peitrine et mamelle* differently; uses different terms for the nostrils in both French and English; differentiates the upper and lower lips of the mouth; elaborates on the parts and form of the hand; and does not witness some of the idiosyncratic terms found in Harley 219 and CUL Add. 8870, e.g., *mahutres* and *lene*. See Skeat, 'Nominale sive Verbale', ll. 25–76. There are certain similarities, but the Harley 219 and CUL Add. 8870 sections are more like each other than similar to the 'Nominale sive Verbale'.

[78] Baker, 'A French Vocabulary', p. 82.
[79] Baker, 'A French Vocabulary', p. 82.
[80] Baker, 'A French Vocabulary', p. 82.

with other words that can be defined by Latin *aries* (a non-castrated ram), but both Hoccleve and the Cambridge scribe place these words together as close enough to be defined by one term (Harley 219, fols 150ᵛ, 151ʳ; CUL Add. 8870, fols 31ʳ, 31ᵛ).[81] They also combine the same French pronouns and nouns: *ma lene* adds a possessive pronoun onto a French noun *aine* (thigh or groin) that already contained the article *la* appended in the source (as *laine* or *lene*); *noruez* represents a corruption of *une orvez* (a snake) (Harley 219, fols 150ʳ, 151ʳ; CUL Add. 8870, fols 30ʳ, 31ᵛ). While entries like *une norvez* may suggest dictation and mishearing as a plausible cause for the reading found in a shared source, most 'errors' seem instead to result from misreading, miscopying or other common lexical adjustments, like the lexicalized article in *ma lene*.[82]

For all the shared content, though, Hoccleve's glossary avoids a number of copying mistakes committed by the Cambridge scribe. The Harley 219 glossary also contains words omitted in CUL Add. 8870 that are found in other Bibbesworth-derived manuscripts, like *palevole*, the term for ladybird unusual enough in French or English (i.e., not clearly defined in the MED, AND or DMF) that Hoccleve surely found it in his source rather than conjuring it from thin air (fol. 151ʳ).[83] Due to a number of copying errors in CUL Add. 8870 but not in Harley 219 and due to the truncated content in Harley 219 while CUL Add. 8870 provides a fuller list of material expected in the *Tretiz* tradition, neither glossary could be the source for the other (and the CUL Add. 8870 is

---

[81] Hoccleve brackets *brinde* and *frein* together with gloss *frenum* (fol. 150ᵛ); CUL Add. 8870 appears to define only *brinde* as *frenum*, with *freint pur un mulet* on the following line, seemingly without definition, though perhaps it was intended to be covered by the previous gloss. CUL Add. 8870 glosses *veruis* and *collart* (which are bracketed together) with *veruex anglice vedure*, with *chastre* (castrated sheep) on a different line with the gloss *aries* (a ram, not castrated), followed by *moton* with the gloss *idem est*, pointing to the prior definition. Baker, 'A French Vocabulary', p. 91 nn. 43–44, notes that *aries* is mistakenly placed next to *chastre* and should belong with the previous terms, while *moton* is linked to *aries* and *veruex* elsewhere. Hoccleve efficiently and indiscriminately glosses all four French words as *aries*. Perhaps each copyist had a confusing source.

[82] See AND, s.v., *aine²*, which notes that the term with lexicalized article is found in the 1396 *Manière de langage*. While *lene* might be identified as an error, it is a variant produced by a common lexical change.

[83] See note 48 above, p. xxviii. See also TL, s.v., *palevole*.

probably the later of the two manuscripts).[84] My theory is that, somewhere up the line, the two texts share a lost source and that Hoccleve innovated beyond the content he found, while the Cambridge scribe mainly copied (and committed far more errors).[85] Hoccleve's intriguing restructuring also suggests that he is working from textual sources, but that does not exclude the possibility that memory of prior rote learning from a written source may have affected some of the choices in the glossary.[86]

Hoccleve's Innovations in Structure and Recorded Language

Compared to most other late medieval *nominalia*, Hoccleve's glossary stands out in its organization and attention to scribal issues that would be relevant for clerical colleagues. Immediately striking is the initial organization: the glossary appears to collate multiple sources into groups in alphabetical order based on the first word in a group. The words on the opening folio 147^v belong to various parts of speech – adjectives, adverbs, noun, preposition, verbs – and are not thematically related, except for the synonyms grouped with each initial headword. The impulses to alphabetize all parts of speech together and provide French synonyms seem unusual.[87] I posit Hoccleve himself as responsible for this reordering, in part because of one word shared only with CUL Add. 8870, *boterel*, glossed as *boviculus* (Harley 219, fol. 147^v; CUL Add. 8870, fol. 31^r). The expected term would be *bovicle* or *bouvelet* (steer),

---

[84] Baker, 'A French Vocabulary', p. 81.

[85] Baker, 'A French Vocabulary', p. 82, notes the general carelessness of the Cambridge scribe, including many errors even in English that cannot be explained as variants, e.g., *dgldfynch* for *goldfinch*. Hoccleve avoids some of these, either through omission or presenting a recognizable term.

[86] On rote learning as a technique used in French learning, see the dialogue in the *Liber Donati* (Critten, *French Lessons*, pp. 54–59), where a young boy must demonstrate the French he has learned and rattles off a list of words similar but not identical to those in Bibbesworth and also Hoccleve's glossary. See also Critten, 'French Didactics', pp. 33–51.

[87] The *Liber Donati*, in Critten, *French Lessons*, pp. 37–38, offers a short list of alphabetized verb infinitives but groups other parts of speech elsewhere; Palsgrave, *Lesclarcissement*, alphabetizes substantial lists of words but always groups them by part of speech.

and the surprising variant *boterel* (which means a small barrel or a toad) has not been found elsewhere or explained satisfactorily. If it is not a copying or placement error, *boterel* could be a playful verbal noun that uses the verb *boter* (to push, strike, shove) to acknowledge a common young bull's activity with the suffix *-el*; or it might derive from a source in which *boterel* is linked to its primary French definition *petit tonneau* (a small barrel), which is misread as *petit taureau* (a small bull).[88] Without context or other attestations, it is difficult to be sure. In Hoccleve's glossary, it appears among words for bakers, entrails and heresy, so there is no thematic reason for its placement. It should almost certainly 'belong' on Harley 219's fols 150ᵛ–151ʳ, where all the other animals shared with CUL Add. 8870 appear. Hoccleve therefore seems to draw on a wordlist like the one in CUL Add. 8870, but only selectively. He also truncates contents but not so much that one could posit a lost folio or quire in his source. If Hoccleve's sources were not themselves incomplete or mangled, then he deliberately reorganizes their elements to compile this list. However, such reorganization is a massive task, one that he eventually abandons in favor of a mixed ordering that is sometimes alphabetical, sometimes thematic, and overall indicative of combining multiple sources.

After having given up alphabetical ordering on fol. 148ʳ, Hoccleve resumes an alphabetical ordering in the middle of 148ᵛ through 149ᵛ for an extended and unusual list of homonyms or near homonyms. Hoccleve's list exhibits a mentality resembling Bibbesworth's pause to clarify ambiguous words, but he goes far beyond the *Tretiz* and its analogous wordlists in both length and depth. While his predecessors focused on words that could be aurally confused, Hoccleve is equally attuned to words that might be misunderstood visually in a manuscript context. One series on fol. 148ᵛ reminds us that medieval scribes could be challenged by minims and *per*, *par* and *pro* manuscript abbreviations, content potentially useful for clerks (italics indicate expansions of abbreviations):

---

[88] DMF, s.v., *boterel¹* and *boterel²*. See also DMF, s.v., *bouvelet* and *bovicle*, and AND, s.v., *boter²*. Baker, 'A French Vocabulary', pp. 82 and 91, identifies *boterel* as an error for *bovicle* or *bovet* and traces it to *boterel* (toad). Because of this word's unusual form and definition, it may help scholars trace the source for these glossaries.

> espernir – spernere   (to despise/reject with scorn)
> esparnir – parcere (to spare)
> esperuer – a sperhauke   (a sparrowhawk)
> esprouer – approbare   (to prove)

Within the *nominalia* tradition, this untitled section might be called 'Verba equivoca' ('Ambiguous words'), but Hoccleve reserves that title for the next section that follows on fol. 149^v. The list of homonyms likely derives from one glossary (or may even have been compiled by Hoccleve) and the formally identified 'Verba equivoca' from another source.[89] Including CUL Add. 8870, that means that Hoccleve uses at least three different sources, probably more, when one considers the breaks and resumption of alphabetical order, the repetition of words in different sections (e.g., *aval* on fols 147^v and 149^v; *roigne* on fols 148^v and 149^v), and the range of words found in his glossary. Even though Hoccleve has multiple sources, his terms are all general – not legal or related to Privy Seal work – supporting the suggestion that clerical men for whom French was a professional necessity may also have been interested in resources that might support broader competencies in the speaking, reading and writing of the language.

So far, I have focused on the practical contents of the glossary, to which might be added the moments when Hoccleve provides conjugations for irregular verbs (e.g., *boelt, chioit, dors,* on fol. 148^v) and various uses of *faire* (fols 148^v and 150^r). But Hoccleve offers unexpected content, too, plausibly drawing on a poet's interest in language. However, it is impossible to ascertain whether Hoccleve might have innovated terms not attested elsewhere, because unusual entries could represent slang or oral usage not otherwise recorded.[90] My point in

---

[89] Another sign that Hoccleve has consulted textual sources and may be compiling independently are mismatched entry words and glosses, e.g., *fluir* (to flourish) glossed with English terms that correspond to its antonym *flenir* (to wither and fade).

[90] The caution by Durkin, *Borrowed Words*, pp. 228–29, is an apt reminder that the first recorded instance of a term should not be assumed to be its first usage or record of its invention. On the other hand, I am not reading this specific Harley 219 glossary as intended as a reference manual for wider audiences in the same way that *Femina*, 'Nominale sive Verbale', and other wordlists were; rather, this manuscript seems to have been produced by and kept within the coterie of

calling attention to these items is to emphasize that Anglo-French was a living and legitimate language for its medieval users; modern lexicography is a monumental task, and scholars may not yet have recognized all the terms collected in Hoccleve's glossary as Anglo-French, but their record in Harley 219 suggests they had some value or currency. Still, some entries offer challenges to modern readers. Hoccleve appears to record the first usage of *compasser* and *deporter* as verbs meaning 'to suffer', grouped into one entry along with more common terms *souffrer* and *endurer* (fol. 147^v). The French *compasser* most often means 'to measure' (either to measure out or measure with a compass), 'to circle' or figuratively 'to concern'; modern dictionaries of medieval and early modern language do not attest 'to suffer' in Continental Frenches or Anglo-French.[91] Hoccleve's *compasser* could be constructing a verb from available noun and adjective forms that did refer to distressing emotions. But *deporter* is more distant from 'to suffer': it would commonly mean 'to exile', 'to deprive (of)' or 'to spare, do without' — all of which might be associated with suffering but none of which denote 'to suffer'.[92] It is plausible that *pati* should have been used to gloss only *souffrer* and *endurer*, and the easiest solution would be attributing the puzzling appearance of *deporter* to an error in copying or organization by Hoccleve or a scribe earlier in the textual transmission, but I am not completely convinced, especially since Hoccleve later glosses *compasser*

Privy Seal clerks who produced its other texts (see above on audience, pp. xxi–xxiii), so any innovations in language or meaning could constitute usages relevant to this manuscript's particular audience, as I posit below for the final entries in the phrasebook.

[91] There are further specialized uses, but most relate to these above concepts, and none denote or connote 'to suffer'. See, for example, DMF, s.v. *compasser* (v.). In addition, I have consulted the AND, *Trésor de la langue Française informatisé*, Godefroy (*Dictionnaire* and *Complément*), Tobler-Lommatzsch *Altfranzösisches Wörterbuch, Französisches Etymologisches Wörterbuch* and Cotgrave, *Dictionarie of the French and English Tongues*. See also, Hoccleve's glossary, fol. 149^v, which glosses *compasser* with the French terms *soeffrer* and *penser*, where *penser* evokes a wide range of concepts associated with 'to think' that can include imagining, conceiving of, being mindful of and thinking things over (AND, s.v., *penser*) – a sense broadly compatible with an intellectual measuring.

[92] See DMF, s.v., *déporter*; AND, s.v., *desporter*. Alternate meanings could denote even acts of comfort, cheer, or enjoyment – quite the opposite of suffering.

among ambiguous words with the French term *soeffrer* (fol. 149ᵛ, col. 3). Three of the four terms could be glossed by Latin *pati* without significant mental gymnastics, and Hoccleve's bracket clearly binds all four terms to each other and to *pati*. This grouping also appears in the section that gathers words under an alphabetical headword, and there is some evidence that Hoccleve or his source attempts to reorganize an earlier wordlist (due to the migration of *boterel*, mentioned above). Thus, no term should be placed here without a corresponding synonymous headword beginning with *C*, and *compasser* is that headword, with the other terms assembled below it. Even if, as a modern reader, I am uncertain of the rationale behind this grouping, Hoccleve's glossary may suggest that medieval readers could see the words as related, even if not exact synonyms.

Further examples record additional experimentation with roots and affixes. The words *enchantour*, *enfementer* and *erbuse* are glossed with *incantator* (fol. 148ʳ), but only *enchantour* is defined as 'enchanter' in existing dictionaries. The two nouns *enfementer* and *erbuse* seem to be based in other French concepts about magic. Godefroy records a masculine noun, *faement*, meaning enchantment, and defines the adverb *féement* as 'by the effect of magic'.[93] Thus, *enfementer* perhaps indicates someone who accomplishes deeds through magic.[94] Similarly, the root of *erbuse* relates to herbs, and the closest analogue is *herbier*, someone who prepares and sells medicinal herbs or a botanist; given the root, context and feminine ending, *erbuse* could refer to a woman who uses herbs to magical ends.[95] The lack of these terms' appearance in modern dictionaries does not render them illegitimate – on the contrary, the Harley 219 evidence helps refine our modern understanding of the terms and constructions that were possible in Anglo-French.

---

[93] Godefroy, *Dictionnaire*, s.v. *faement* (n.) and s.v. *faeement* (adv.); see also DMF, s.v. *féement* (adv.).

[94] I assume that the term is a noun based on its companions and gloss, even though the form resembles a French infinitive.

[95] See, for example, AND, s.v. *herbe* (n.), *herbai* (n.), *herbu* (adj.); DMF, s.v. *herbier¹* (n.). Misogynist assumptions about women may also apply, if one thinks of medieval (and post-medieval) treatments of Circe and Morgan le Fay.

Hoccleve also experiments with mild scatology, perhaps for the entertainment of his audience, and comic and even vulgar content was not uncommon in language learning materials.[96] One series in his semi-alphabetical section seems constructed to elicit an amused reaction (fol. 148^v):

creuer – crepare	(to burst)
forscrier – exclamar*e*	(to cry out)
chier – caccare	(to defecate)
chioit – caccavit	(he defecated)
chatiller – to tikele	(to tickle)

The first three infinitives mean to burst, to cry out and to defecate, with the conjugation of the irregular verb included, no doubt, for readerly edification. They are followed by *chatiller* (to excite or to tickle) whose gloss *to tikele* switches to the Middle English, perhaps to amuse the reader; the secondary definition of *tikelen* is 'to cause delight'.[97]

Hoccleve additionally offers inventive fart words, which is of course edifying in terms of Chaucerian, earthy content but also for connecting Hoccleve to CUL Add. 8870 and for considering the multilingual nature of his glossing practice:

| vener ⎫ | fetare an^{ce} | |
| vesser ⎭ | fyste | (fol. 148^r) |

The most easily identifiable terms are *vesser* and *fyste*. The linking of French, AND s.v., *vessir* (to fart) and Middle English, MED, s.v., *fist*, n.2 (fart), suggests that *vener* should be related. It might be an alternative spelling for *venter*, which can mean 'to make wind', although that usage typically has a meteorological sense. The term can also mean 'to blow', and the *Tretiz* uses *venter* for 'blowing a horn' when hunting, a sense that might be transferred to flatulence, especially in a Middle English context

---

[96] See Critten, 'Practising', pp. 929–31.

[97] DMF, s.v. *chatoiller*, and MED, s.v., *tikelen*, both can also mean 'to arouse', which may take the joke a step further.

where the etymological root of *fist* is 'blowing'.⁹⁸ Additionally, in Anglo-French, *vent* could take on the meaning 'empty words' in legal texts.⁹⁹ In the hands of a poet familiar with Chaucer's *Summoner's Tale*, embracing a translation that turns empty speech into farting seems plausible. Hoccleve's would be the first record of the verb used to indicate the breaking of wind.¹⁰⁰

The gloss then must also denote or connote 'to fart', but it can only be understood through interpretation of Latin and Middle English together. Curiously, this entry is the only one in Harley 219 with an abbreviation for *anglice*, the term glossaries commonly used to identify the glossing language as English.¹⁰¹ In CUL Add. 8870, by comparison, the scribe assiduously announces shifts to English with *anglice*, abbreviated *aᵉ*. In Harley 219, Hoccleve follows a precedent exhibited consistently in CUL Add. 8870, and likely in their shared source, to announce the language change with *anᶜᵉ*.¹⁰² But Hoccleve only does so when it is essential to understanding a multilingual gloss in which the Latin and English offer not competing or alternative linguistic glosses but rather one gloss consisting of a Latin infinitive and Middle English direct

---

⁹⁸⁾ DMF, s.v., *venter*, for intransitive uses offers 'faire du vent' (to make wind) (I.A) or 'souffler' (to blow) (I.B); 'wind' in the attestations in Godefroy, *Complément*, s.v., *venter*, focus on meteorological occurrences. I thank Thomas Hinton (personal correspondence) for conversations about these topics. Cotgrave's 1611 dictionary attests *venne* as 'A fizzle, or small fyste', and *venneur* as 'A fizzler, or fyster', indicating that *vener* could be understood as a root for these words. Claudius Hollyband's 1580 dictionary lists *venne* and *vesse* as synonymous with 'fart' but provides no similar attestation for *vener* or *venter* (though he does helpfully provide the conjugation for *vessir* and sentence structure for calling someone 'a great farter or fyster' or 'an olde man or woman, which doth nothing but fyste'). See also MED, s.v., *fist*, n.2.

⁹⁹⁾ AND, s.v., *vent¹*, def. 4.

¹⁰⁰⁾ TLF, s.v. *venter*, def. A.2.b, gives an attestation in Zola in the late nineteenth century.

¹⁰¹⁾ See p. xxxvii and n.75, above.

¹⁰²⁾ The practice of denoting the glossing language was common; see Cannon, *From Literacy to Literature*, pp. 28–29.

object.[103] The Latin term *fetare* means 'to bring forth', 'to give birth' or 'to breed', thus producing the meaning 'to bring forth a fart' or 'to give birth to a fart'.[104] It is also but one vowel away from *fetere* (to stink). Why offer this multilingual gloss instead of simply using one Latin or English word? We might see this entry and gloss as resembling the trilingual riddles that could be used as elements of rhetorical training, like those identified by Andrew Galloway in the *Secretum philosophorum* and various lyrics in London, British Library, MS Harley 2253, in which the reader must be sufficiently versed in all three languages to enjoy the playful content.[105] The notion of giving birth to a fart may seem surprising, but 'to breed a fart' was apparently idiomatic by 1611: alongside *vessir* as 'to fyste, to let a fyste', Cotgrave defines *vessesier* as 'To breed a fyste, to make breakewind, or let a fyste'.[106] Hoccleve's glossary offers an even earlier attestation of the English phrase.

Whether these inventive usages can be attributed to our poet or simply to his milieu cannot be determined, since first written attestations cannot indicate whether words, phrases or proverbs, for instance, were circulating orally. Whether Hoccleve found inspiration for these items in a source, heard them on the street or invented them, his recording them in Harley 219 shows his awareness of language, and some of the more creative elements might even be evidence of his working through how one traverses across languages and from literal to figurative language, as practice in the creation of poetic usages.

---

[103] Hoccleve's English infinitives almost always contain 'to' as a marker, which further supports reading 'fyste' as a noun.

[104] LSLD, s.v., *feto*; see also du Cange, s.v., *fetare*. To 'breed' here refers to the act of producing or bringing something (usually a child) forward from conception to birth (OED, s.v., *breed* v., I.1.a).

[105] Andrew Galloway, 'The Rhetoric of Riddling in Late Medieval England: The 'Oxford' Riddles, the *Secretum philosophorum*, and the Riddles in *Piers Plowman*', *Speculum*, 70 (1995), pp. 68–105 (pp. 82–84), discusses riddles as part of educational training and points to some trilingual riddles.

[106] Cotgrave, s.v., *vessir* and *vessesier*. The list of fart terms and phrases beginning with '*vess-*' in Cotgrave is surprisingly detailed. Some of the entries, like *vessir*, have precedent in Hollyband's *A dictionarie*, but not *vessesier*.

A Posited Connection between Hoccleve's Glossary and CUL Add. 8870

If I am correct that Hoccleve's glossary and CUL Add. 8870 have a shared source, then the latter manuscript may provide some clues as to how these two glossaries are the product of a similar group of London clerks. CUL Add. 8870 has been described by Baker as a legal notebook because virtually all of its contents relate to the practice of law: legal statutes, multiple Latin mnemonics, tracts and notes on *essoins* (excuses for not appearing in court) and conveyancing (the transfer of property), the Latin legal glossary *Expositio vocabulorum* and a variety of miscellaneous notes.[107] The first two gatherings (fols 1–14 and 15–28) are on parchment, written primarily in the same Anglicana hand, and they contain a variety of tracts listed in the table to the volume on fol. 1ʳ; fol. 29 has been removed, and only a stub remains, where presumably the final entry listed in the table but no longer extant had once resided.[108] The main hand is early fifteenth century and the product of formal clerical training: it is neat and regular, and it contains letter forms often found in Chancery documents. On fol. 13ʳ, a note in a second, more informal Anglicana hand is added, and this hand may plausibly be

---

[107] For the full list of the manuscript's tracts and notes, see J. H. Baker, with J. S. Ringrose, *A Catalogue of English Legal Manuscripts in Cambridge University Library* (Boydell and Brewer, 1996), pp. 633–41, and 'A French Vocabulary', pp. 80–81. J. R. Mattison notes that the limp parchment bindings for the manuscript indicate 'a homemade production' and contain erasures (private correspondence); J. H. Baker suggests that the one erasure that reads *summa viij* may indicate that the parchment may have been reused from an old account roll (private correspondence). To my eye, the upper erasure appears to read 'De' followed by illegible letters. I am grateful to J. R. Mattison for sharing photos of the bindings and to both Baker and Mattison for conversations about this manuscript.

[108] In assigning both quires to the same main hand, I differ from Baker, 'A French Vocabulary', p. 80, who sees different hands active in each gathering; in my view, the letter forms are consistent across the folios and in the table to the volume (particularly *D, d*, rounded *e* and *E, g* and *W* in both heading script and circular *W*), which suggests one creator of both the quires and the table. Both quires also have the same layout of 51 lines of text, although the second has been rubricated while the first only has spaces and guide letters. The table names the missing text 'statutus de clementibus'.

identified with the main hand of the third gathering, including the French glossary.[109] The third and fourth gatherings are on paper, and the fourth appears to be in yet another fifteenth-century Anglicana hand, and 'bound in so as to be read by reversing the volume'.[110] This evidence suggests that at least the first three gatherings, and probably the entire contents, were at one point together and in the possession of the same medieval owner.

Little is known about the manuscript's medieval provenance, but most of the clues provided are in the third gathering: mention of 'Ricardus Ebor. archiepiscopus' in a tract on fol. 36^r; a reference to a case in 1388 on fol. 49^r; and a note on the sealing of the will and testament of Robert Clopton, alderman, before the London Lord Mayor and another alderman on fol. 55^r. The archbishop of York could be either Richard Scrope (1398–1405) or Richard Flemyng (1424–25).[111] Clopton died in 1448, but the Clopton note appears to have been added in a slightly later hand.[112] There is another vague reference, 'quod Hore' after

---

[109] This note is 'Quot modis dicitur excec' (sic: exceptio). This script is more formal than the more current execution of the scribe in the third gathering, but the forms of a, d, g, p, tall s and others, plus a general preference for thicker strokes in the back of the a, f, p and tall s and the use of a similar symbol (resembling modern infinity) at the conclusion of a text (cf. fol. 51^r) suggest the plausibility that they may be written by the same individual. There is another version of this statute on fols 22^{r-v} with substantial textual differences.

[110] Baker, 'A French Vocabulary', p. 81, notes the positioning of the quires; in *Catalogue*, p. 640, he additionally notes that the paper in quire three contains the watermark of a hunting horn, which is also found in quire four, along with a bull's head watermark.

[111] Baker, 'A French Vocabulary', p. 80–81.

[112] It exhibits, for instance, the circular *C* with a vertical slash through it and the ill-formed *h* that descends below the line that are indicative of late secretary hands and often seen in sixteenth-century secretary. Based on the overall letter forms, these in particular and the *Cl* ligature, I would tentatively suggest that the later additions on both fol. 13^v ('Feodum militare et hida') and fol. 55^r (the Clopton note) are in the same hand because they tend to match in form and aspect. Baker, *Catalogue*, pp. 633 and 639, dates the script to the later fifteenth century and the reign of Henry VI. For Clopton, a member of the Drapers' Company, see Josiah C. Wedgwood, *History of Parliament: Biographies of the Members of the Commons House, 1439–1509* (H. M. Stationery Office, 1936), p.

a note on fol. 49ᵛ. Baker notes that Hore might have been Robert Hore, the filazer of the King's Bench from 1399–1432.[113] This internal evidence places the quire's contents to between 1388 and the 1430s, leading Baker to date the manuscript to the first half of the fifteenth century.

My interpretation of the last clue supports this broad date. There is a final oblique reference in this gathering: the colophon to the French phrasebook 'quod T amen pur charite B' on fol. 35ʳ. These initials 'T. B.', when considered alongside a note in the fourth gathering, offer intriguing possibilities. Baker proposes that 'T. B.' might be Sir Thomas Burdet of Arrow, Warwickshire, who was knighted before December 1392 and whose name appears in a deed granting him a pension from the Prior of Studley, nearby in Warwickshire, on fol. 65ᵛ, though Baker acknowledges that there is no evidence that Sir Thomas studied law, implying that the knight would have had little interest in the other contents of the volume.[114]

However, there is another possibility: another Thomas Burdet was a clerk of the Privy Seal named with Thomas Hoccleve in a grant of 23 July 1401.[115] He does not appear elsewhere alongside Hoccleve or other royal clerks for good reason: by 4 August 1401, he was fortunate enough to be referred to as a 'king's clerk' and appointed rector of Aston

---

199; Wedgwood proposes that Clopton may not have been from Clopton, Warwickshire. This manuscript has connections to Warwickshire, so perhaps some link of Clopton to the region may not be ruled out. The note might have been preserved either due to the copyist's relationship with Clopton, or as a record of the powers given to the Lord Mayor and Aldermen in the mid-fifteenth century.

[113] Baker, *Catalogue*, p. 641; see also C. A. F. Meekings, 'A King's Bench Bill Formulary', *Journal of Legal History*, 6 (1985), pp. 86–104 (p. 104n.8), for Hore's service.

[114] Baker, 'A French Vocabulary', pp. 80–81. In fact, Sir Thomas Burdet, who died in 1442, is described as having a record of violent temperament, disrespect for the law, and criminal acts, even when he served as Sheriff, in 'Burdet, Sir Thomas (d. 1442), of Arrow, Warws'., in *The History of Parliament: the House of Commons 1386-1421*, ed. J. S. Roskell, L. Clark, C. Rawcliffe (1993), online <http://www.historyofparliamentonline.org/volume/1386-1421/member/burdet-sir-thomas-1442> [accessed 2 September 2021].

[115] Burrow, *Thomas Hoccleve*, p. 3,5 no. 9; Brown, 'The Privy Seal Clerks', p. 262n2.

Cantlow in Warwickshire (some five or six miles from Arrow), a prized, permanent benefice.[116] Unfortunately, Rector Thomas died by 1403, and his replacement was named by the Prior of Studley.[117] His will demonstrates connections to St. Mary le Strand and Westminster Chapel, both in London, suggesting that the rector and Privy Seal clerk were indeed the same man.[118] Thus the 'T. B.' on fol. 35ʳ could refer to Rector Thomas, plausibly a son or kinsman of Sir Thomas of Arrow, the latter of whom may have had the influence to secure his clerical relative a benefice near their home.[119] As Kathryn Kerby-Fulton observes, benefices (let alone permanent ones) were difficult to secure, and the first advancement for clerks was often not a rectorship but instead a more minor position.

---

[116] See R. S. Mylne, *The Canon Law* (Morrison and Gibb, 1912), p. 152; *Calendar of the Patent Rolls Preserved in the Public Record Office: 1399–1401*, ed. by H. C. Maxwell Lyte (H. M. Stationery Office, 1903), pp. 513 and 527, where Burdet is identified as a 'king's clerk'. As Kathryn Kerby-Fulton, *Clerical Proletariat*, pp. 2–4, 28–29, notes, only rectors had permanent tenure, and the elevation to such positions was a rare achievement in the later Middle Ages. And, of course, Hoccleve admits that he gave up hoping for a benefice and resigned himself to marriage in *Regiment of Princes*, ll. 1447–56. See also Kerby-Fulton, *Clerical Proletariat*, pp. 110–39.

[117] 'Parishes: Aston Cantlow', in *A History of the County of Warwick: Volume 3, Barlichway Hundred*, ed. Philip Styles (London: Victoria County History, 1945), pp. 31–42, *British History Online*, http://www.british-history.ac.uk/vch/warks/vol3/pp31-42 [accessed 8 September 2021], suggests that Thomas was presented in 1402 and died in 1403.

[118] London, The National Archives, PROB 11/2A/47. My thanks to Sebastian Sobecki for this reference.

[119] See 'Burdet, Sir Thomas'. When Sir Thomas dies in 1442, he leaves one son and heir, Nicholas, but that does not eliminate the possibility of other sons or kin who predeceased him. Sir Thomas Burdet would have gained influence as part of the affinity of Richard Beauchamp, earl of Warwick; see Christine Carpenter, *Locality and Polity: A Study of Warwickshire Landed Society, 1401–1499* (Cambridge University Press, 1992), e.g., pp. 313–46. The King himself presented clerk Burdet; when the Prior of Studley nominated his replacement, the action should be seen as part of a dispute about the Crown's claim to the advowson, which continued for some years; see 'Parishes: Aston Cantlow', pp. 31–42.

Difficult, that is, unless a clerk had someone influential in his corner, such as a patron or relative.[120]

In my view, the 'T. B.' who provided the source for both the vocabulary and the conversation guide in CUL Add. 8870 should be identified as Thomas Burdet. The clearly negligent errors in the vocabulary and the fact that the hand does not at all resemble the scripts used by Privy Seal clerks indicate that Burdet was not likely to be the copyist but more plausibly the owner of the source, which the scribe of CUL Add. 8870 copied. Perhaps the scribe was another family member or a clerk at Aston Cantlow or Studley who then entered the note concerning Sir Thomas and Studley Priory. Such circumstances would explain how the notes about Sir Thomas and Studley Priory could appear in the same manuscript as the glossary that shares a source with Hoccleve's. Privy Seal clerk then Rector Thomas Burdet provides the site at which Hoccleve's and Sir Thomas Burdet's circles overlap.

The Short Phrasebook in Harley 219

It is not necessarily odd to find a phrasebook accompanying a wordlist, but texts that carry the title *Manière de langage* and other phrasebooks, like the one in CUL Add. 8870, tend to offer practical dialogues instructing readers how to woo a lady, secure lodgings or buy and sell goods, though there is some room for humor and playfulness.[121]

---

[120] Kerby-Fulton, *Clerical Proletariat*, pp. 120–24, addresses the importance of a major patron for securing benefices, which could also include nepotism, in the case of London clerk Thomas Fovent. As Clementine Oliver, 'A Political Pamphleteer in Late Medieval England: Thomas Fovent, Geoffrey Chaucer, Thomas Usk, and the Merciless Parliament of 1388', *New Medieval Literatures*, 5 (2003), pp. 167–98, shows, Fovent was apparently related to a kinswoman and abbess who may have facilitated one of his benefices. While not all individuals given benefices necessarily resided on site, if Burdett were from the area, as seems plausible, that might increase the likelihood of his presence at Aston Cantlow.

[121] Kristol, *Manières de langage*, pp. xvii–xix, explains that the title *Manière de langage* (or *de/du parler*) indicates more of a genre of conversation manual than any one specific base text, hence his edition's plural title *Manières*, because the three manuals edited are reasonably distinct, even if they have common underlying themes and goals. The conversation-guide in CUL Add. 8870 is more typical of the *Manière* genre and shares no content with the phrases in

Although scholars refer to the final selections of Harley 219's glossary, which take up the right 2/3 of on fol. 151ᵛ, as a phrasebook, it is certainly atypical of the genre. It may have been added slightly later, as some entries witness an even more 'current' hand than the one in the rest of the glossary (which is not as formal as Hoccleve's copying of the *Othea*). The contents are disjointed. After four rather pedestrian practical phrases about wiping and drying one's hands, eyes and nose, the French and English terms for an 'ellir tree' intrude, leftovers from the glossary's final column which ends with a list of trees. The next statements are conversational and idiomatic, and they rather unexpectedly subvert the expectations set by the previous lines. Hoccleve presents the French equivalents of 'it is no iape' and 'y dide it maugre my teeth' – perhaps the latter was the refrain of bureaucratic scribes, who were less able to voice Bartleby Scrivener's 'I prefer not to'. The next entries teach readers how to call someone a *froward cherl* in French (likely the last entry in Hoccleve's hand). These entries may even be wry parallels to the preceding practical phrases, suggesting that insistences upon veracity, admissions that tasks were completed under duress and insults may be equally useful for Hoccleve's Privy Seal colleagues.

The final entries on fol. 151ᵛ stray even farther afield. Before they begin, there is a one-line space and another hand, identified by Sobecki as belonging to Privy Seal clerk Richard Priour, makes additional entries, primarily phrases.¹²² One informs readers how to describe a rusty knife blade and how to direct someone to find a body within the tomb. Yet there is an intriguing translation and interlinear addition in the latter

---

Harley 219. The insult in Hoccleve's glossary may have the most precedent in *Manière*-type texts; for more colorful insults in French, *c*. 1399, see Kristol, *Manières*, pp. 54–55, and Critten, 'Practising', pp. 929–31, though none is an exact match for the entry in Harley 219.

[122] Downes, 'A "Frenche booke called the Pistill of Othea"', pp. 759–80, suggests that the final lines are not in the main scribe's hand, and Sobecki, 'Handwriting of Privy Seal Clerks', p. 12, uses detailed paleographical evidence to identify the line translating 'lemele – a blade of a knyf', which appears after a one-line gap, as the beginning of someone else's hand, plausibly Priour's. In 'A New Hoccleve Literary Manuscript', p. 821, I assumed that the final section was Hoccleve's more current hand with some variations. It is difficult to be sure, though I am persuaded by the paleographical evidence that at least the final three lines are another hand.

case. The French 'le corps est souz lame' does not translate to the Middle English 'the body is withynne the toumbe' – 'under the tombstone' would be more accurate, unless we are to read 'lame' as 'l'ame' (soul), in which case, 'the body is beneath the soul' (possibly a consolation evoking the moralistic topos).[123] In the manuscript above *souz* (under, beneath) is written interlinearly *deinz* (inside), perhaps to parallel the Middle English preposition and call attention to the potential for wordplay, since *souz* remains without being canceled. These phrases seem oddly specific and unlikely to be of significant use to a traveler or of much amusement to the casual reader, but perhaps there is a more serious personal and professional significance.

The final eclectic phrases shift toward topics of aging and the passage of time, with the last entry translated as 'while he was there' – evoking further loss it would seem. Whose loss? Sobecki has suggested that these may be the ruminations of one of Hoccleve's colleagues who traveled to France on the king's business during the Hundred Years War.[124] And that may be one purpose, but I want to call attention to the final lines, those likely written in the hand of Richard Priour, Hoccleve's Privy Seal associate:

> Baillez moy mes cafignouns – take me my pynsouns
> Cest chival de lowage – this is an hyred hors
> tantdyz qil y feust – while he was there (fol. 151ᵛ)

I initially suggested that these lines were written by Hoccleve, establishing a link between his work in Harley 219 and the *Letter of Cupid* – where he invents or records for the first time the use of 'hired horse' to call a woman a whore: 'Shee for the rode of folk is so desyrid, / And as an hors fro day to day is hyrid' (ll. 102–3).[125] But if they are indeed in Priour's hand, or any other Privy Seal clerk for that matter, instead we

---

[123] DMF, s.v., *lame¹*, def. C.

[124] Sobecki, *Last Words*, pp. 65–100.

[125] Sobecki, 'Handwriting of Privy Seal Clerks', p. 12.

[125] *Epistle of Cupid*, in *'My Compleinte' and Other Poems*, ed. by Roger Ellis, Exeter Medieval Texts and Studies (University of Exeter Press, 2001), pp. 93–111; Schieberle, 'A New Hoccleve Literary Manuscript', p. 821. But see Downes, 'A "Frenche booke"', for an earlier identification of the hands as distinct.

can see them as memorials. *Baillez* is an unusual verb to use for 'bring me my slippers' – the verb *bailler* does mean 'to give' or 'hand over' but it is commonly used for the delivery of documents, property or official letters (AND, s.v., *bailler*). The use of *baillez* may indicate the clerks' more common usage, but it also evokes the name of John Bailey, the Privy Seal clerk and Hoccleve's close friend who died in 1420.[126] Hoccleve, of course, dies in 1426. These lines may not be in his hand, but they could be arguably equally important, written as a tribute to Hoccleve and perhaps Bailey, after their deaths, when the manuscript passed to the colleagues who helped produce it.

In sum, Hoccleve's glossary and the phrases that follow it highlight the interests of London and Westminster clerks in practicing French – not only for their professional lives but also to promote a broader understanding of the language. More than that, we see on display Hoccleve's sophisticated and complex relationship to language, both with respect to his occupation and his poetic production, potentially considering how to embrace figurative language by recording (or creating?) uncommon terms that draw on expected French forms. And he innovates beyond the typical late medieval wordlist genre by attempting alphabetical organization, combining multiple glossary texts, attending to words that might be confused not only aurally but also visually, and generating an unusual phrasebook. Hoccleve's glossary may not be directed specifically at helping readers appreciate the French literary texts that accompany it in Harley 219, but it promotes a wider understanding of how language works and how multilingual language study could be a source of edification and pleasure.

Editorial Principles

Orthography

The text has been altered as little as possible to preserve Hoccleve's orthographic choices. In the few instances in which intervention has

---

[126] Sobecki, *Last Words*, pp. 69–92, illustrates the close relationship between Hoccleve and Bailey, which includes analysis of Bailey's will and of the *Series* as Hoccleve's attempt to mourn the death a friend and confront his own mortality. I read these lines in Harley 219 as having similar potential to memorialize Bailey and Hoccleve, respectively, for their colleagues.

been necessary, editorial alterations are indicated by square brackets and are explained in the notes. Letters that are often interchangeable such as *i/j* and *u/v* have been printed as they appear in the manuscript.

Punctuation

The manuscript has only two forms of punctuation that are represented in this edition: 1) brackets that connect headwords and 2) virgules that indicate separation between two short headwords on the same line (e.g., 'sot | fol' on fol. 147ᵛ, 'non / nient' on fol. 148ʳ).[127] Since the manuscript's narrow columns are often packed with headwords and glosses, Hoccleve sometimes employs long dashes or virgules to separate headword from gloss, but he is inconsistent (e.g., long dashes appear often in the early folios through 149ᵛ and less commonly later; virgules appear in the list of internal body parts but rarely elsewhere). These dashes or virgules are not represented in the edition. When the manuscript lacks a gloss for a headword, I have used a dash to indicate that absence; there are editorial and not in the manuscript.

I have not introduced modern apostrophes that would indicate elision between articles and nouns in words such as 'leure' (for 'l'eure'), 'cest' (for 'c'est'), 'leschyn' (for 'l'eschyn'), and so on. Nor have I introduced the cedilla (ç) or modern French accent marks indicating pronunciation of vowels, which do not appear in the manuscript.

Manuscript Suspensions and Abbreviations

The expansion of manuscript suspension marks and abbreviations has been indicated with italicized text. I have taken what might be interpreted as a scribal flourish after final *k* and *ll* as indicating an *e*, based on words written out in full that adhere to that convention, e.g., 'Corbelle' (fol. 151ʳ).

Capitalisation and Text Formatting

Majuscule letters have been retained wherever they occur in the manuscript. Capital letters are clearly intentional when written in

---

[127] The manuscript also occasionally uses brackets or long dashes that indicate when a headword or gloss carries over onto the next line, but these are not represented in the edition to avoid confusion with the other brackets and to generate a cleaner text.

headings and in some entries that constitute phrases, but they seem to be less purposefully interspersed among other headwords and glosses; in those less purposeful instances, scribal variation seems the likely cause for capitalisation.

Although I question whether all words can be easily divided by language in a multilingual environment, to facilitate the reading of the glossary, the edition represents French and English vernacular headwords and glosses in lower-case text and represents Latin glosses in small capitals; notes indicate when those distinctions might be debated.

Mise-en-page and Modern Glosses

The layout of Harley 219 is challenging to replicate in a modern edition within the limitations of standard page sizes: Harley 219 presents three columns, each one of which contains Anglo-Norman terms and their Latin and/or Middle English glosses. The edition indicates the Harley 219 folio divisions and column breaks with labels such as 'fol. 151^v' and 'col. 2' when a new folio or column begins. Latin section headings in the manuscript are reproduced and translated. To accommodate the modern reader, the glossary is organised in in three columns that indicate 1) the manuscript's Anglo-French entry word(s), 2) the manuscript's Latin, French or Middle English gloss(es), and 3) a marginal, italicised modern editorial gloss that I have constructed to translate and interpret the manuscript terms.

With regards to the editorial glosses, I hope the dictionary format does not deceive readers: the glosses are my own interpretations, laid out here to give the reader a foothold into beginning to understand the complexities of the medieval document. Producing a modern editorial gloss for each entry often requires succinct definitions for rather complex concepts, and such glosses are always subject to reinterpretation and improvement. I tend to prioritize the glossing language to produce what seem to me to be plausible definitions, but sometimes it has been necessary to extend meanings and attempt to negotiate the space among multiple headwords and a single gloss, or among seemingly disjunctive headwords and glosses. The modern glosses should be taken as conjectural, as starting places rather than the finish line for understanding how these words might have functioned in the trilingual context of late medieval England and the Privy Seal office. I am grateful to the anonymous press reviewer for many suggestions that have improved the glosses and footnotes, but there are certainly stones left unturned, such as a fuller investigation of medieval Latin from the Netherlands as an influence, which the reviewer helpfully suggested but which I was unable to incorporate into my revisions.[128]

Notes to the Edition

Notes attempt to clarify my editorial process of interpretation, suggest any additional meanings or sources that should be considered, and provide other information about manuscript features. Claims that a term has not yet been attested in an online dictionary were acccurate at the time of production but that status may change over time.

Abbreviations

AND	*Anglo-Norman Dictionary*
ANTS	Anglo-Norman Texts Series
Cotgrave	Randle Cotgrave, *A Dictionarie of the French and English Tongues* (London, 1611)
DMF	*Dictionnaire du Moyen Français (1330–1500)*
DMLBS	*Dictionary of Medieval Latin from British Sources*
Du Cange	Du Cange, et al., *Glossarium mediae et infimae latinitatis* (L. Favre, 1883–1887)
EEBO	*Early English Books Online*
FEW	*Französisches Etymologisches Wörterbuch*
Godefroy	*Le Dictionnaire de l'ancienne langue française* (and *Complément*)
LSLD	*A New Latin Dictionary*, ed. by Charlton T. Lewis and Charles Short (Harper and Brothers, 1891)
MED	*Middle English Dictionary*
MLR	*Modern Language Review*
NQ	*Notes and Queries*
OED	*Oxford English Dictionary*
OFrD	*Old French-English Dictionary*, ed. by Alan Hindley, and others (Cambridge University Press, 2006)
RES	*Review of English Studies*

---

[128] See *Lexicon latinitatis nederlandicae medii aevi*, 6 vols, ed by J. W. Fuchs and Olga Weijers (Brill, 1977–2005).

SAC   Studies in the Age of Chaucer
STC   Short-Title Catalogue, 2nd ed.
TL   Tobler-Lommatzsch, Altfranzösisches Wörterbuch
TLL   Tony Hunt, Teaching and Learning Latin in Thirteenth-Century England, 3 vols (Brewer, 1991)
TLF   Trésor de la langue Française informatisé

Works Cited

Manuscripts

Cambridge, Cambridge University Libraries, MS Additional 8870
London, British Library, MS Harley 219
Stockholm, Kungliga Biblioteket, MS Vu 22

Dictionaries

Anglo-Norman Dictionary, https://anglo-norman.net/ [accessed 1 November 2021]
Cotgrave, Randle. *A Dictionarie of the French and English Tongues* (London, 1611). Early English Books Online, https://proquest.libguides.com/eebopqp/ [accessed 1 November 2021]
Dictionnaire de l'ancienne langue française et de tous ses dialectes du IXe au XVe siècle, and Complément, ed. by Frédéric Eugène Godefroy (Paris: F. Vieweg, 1880–1902), https://www.lexilogos.com/francais_ancien.htm/ [accessed 1 November 2021]
Dictionary of Medieval Latin from British Sources, ed. by David Howlett and others (Oxford University Press, 1975-2013). Logeion, https://logeion.uchicago.edu/lexidium/ [accessed 1 November 2021]
Dictionnaire du Moyen Français (1330–1500), version 2020, http://zeus.atilf.fr/dmf/ [accessed 1 November 2021]
Du Cange, Charles du Fresne, sieur, et al., *Glossarium mediae et infimae latinitatis* (Niort: L. Favre, 1883–1887)
Französisches Etymologisches Wörterbuch, ed. by W. von Wartburg and others, https://lecteur-few.atilf.fr/index.php/ [accessed 1 November 2021]

Lexicon latinitatis nederlandicae medii aevi, ed. J. W. Fuchs and others, 11 vols (Leiden: Brill, 1977)

Middle English Dictionary Online, ed. by Hans Kurath and others (Ann Arbor: University of Michigan Press, 1952–2001) https://quod.lib.umich.edu/m/middle-english-dictionary/ [accessed 1 November 2021]

A New Latin Dictionary, ed. by Charlton T. Lewis and Charles Short (London: Harper and Brothers, 1891)

Oxford English Dictionary (online), September 2021 (Oxford University Press), https://www-oed-com [accessed 1 November 2021]

Old French-English Dictionary, ed. by Alan Hindley and others (Cambridge University Press, 2006)

Tobler-Lommatzsch: Altfranzösisches Wörterbuch, ed. by Adolf Tobler and Erhard Lommatzsch (Stuttgart: F. Steiner, 1925–1995), http://as-bwc-tl.spdns.org/tl/ocr/index.html/ [accessed 1 November 2021]

Trésor de la langue Française informatisé, http://www.atilf.fr/tlfi [accessed 1 November 2021]

Primary Works

Alumni Oxonienses, 1500–1714 (Oxford, 1891), available at *British History Online*, https://www.british-history.ac.uk/alumni-oxon/1500-1714/pp29-50 [accessed 4 April 2024]

Baker, J. H. 'A French Vocabulary and Conversation-Guide in a Fifteenth-Century Legal Notebook', *Medium Aevum*, 58 (1989), pp. 80–102

Bentley, Elna Jean Young, 'The *Formulary* of Thomas Hoccleve' (unpublished doctoral dissertation, Emory University, 1965)

Calendar of the Patent Rolls Preserved in the Public Record Office: 1399–1401, ed. H. C. Maxwell-Lyte (London: H. M. Stationery Office, 1903)

Christine de Pizan, *Christine de Pizan: Epistre Othea*, ed. by Gabriella Parussa (Geneva: Droz, 1999)

Critten, Rory G., *French Lessons in Late-Medieval England: The Liber donati and Commune parlance* (Leeds: Arc Humanities Press, 2023)

Cotgrave, Randle, *Dictionarie of the French and English Tongues* (London, 1611), *STC*, 2nd ed., 5830
Hoccleve, Thomas, *'My Compleinte' and Other Poems*, ed. by Roger Ellis (University of Exeter Press, 2001)
——. *Regiment of Princes*, ed. by Charles R. Blyth (Kalamazoo, MI: Medieval Institute Press, 1999)
Hunt, Tony, 'The Anglo-Norman Vocabularies in MS Oxford, Bodleian Library, Douce 88', *Medium Aevum*, 49 (1980), pp. 5–25
—— (ed.), *Teaching and Learning Latin in Thirteenth-Century England*, 3 vols (Cambridge: D. S. Brewer, 1991)
——, 'The Trilingual Vocabulary in MS Westminster Abbey 34/11', *Notes and Queries*, 226 (1981), pp. 14–15
Hollyband, Claudius, *A Dictionarie French and English* (London, 1593), *STC*, 2nd ed., 6737
——, *The treasurie of the French tong* (London, 1580), *STC*, 2nd ed., 6761
Gessler, Jean (ed.), *Manière de langage qui enseigne à bien parler et écrire le français: modèles de conversations composés en Angleterre a la fin du XIVe siecle* (Brussels: Édition Universelle – Paris: Droz, 1934)
Kristol, Andres M. (ed.), *Manières de langage (1396, 1399, 1415)*, Anglo-Norman Texts 53 (London: Anglo-Norman Text Society, 1995)
Learning French in Medieval England: The Manuscripts of Walter de Bibbesworth's 'Tretiz', directed by Thomas Hinton (University of Exeter), https://tretiz.exeter.ac.uk/ [accessed 30 July 2021]
Liber Donati, ed. by Brian Merrilees and Beata Sitarz-Fitzpatrick, Plain Texts Series 9 (London: Anglo-Norman Text Society, 1993)
Orthographia Gallica, ed. by R. C. Johnston, Plain Texts Series 5 (London: Anglo-Norman Text Society, 1987)
Owen, Annie (ed.), *Le Traitié de Walter de Bibbesworth sur la langue française* (Paris: Presses Universitaires de France, 1929)
Palsgrave, John, *Lesclarcissement de la langue francoyse* (London, 1530), *STC*, 2nd ed., 19166
Le Secret des Secrets: Traduction du X^{ve} siècle, ed. by Denis Lorée (Paris: Honoré Champion, 2017)
Rothwell, William (ed.), *Femina (Trinity College, Cambridge MS B.14.40)*, Anglo-Norman On-Line Hub, 2005, https://

anglo-norman.net/wp-content/uploads/2021/07/femina.pdf/ [accessed 15 May 2024]

Skeat, W. W. (ed.), 'Nominale sive Verbale', *Transactions of the Philological Society* (1906), pp. 1*–50*

Walter de Bibbesworth: Le Tretiz, ed. by William Rothwell, Anglo-Norman Online Hub, 2009, https://anglo-norman.net/wp-content/uploads/2021/07/bibb-gt.pdf/ [accessed 15 May 2024]

Secondary Works

Adams, J. N. *The Latin Sexual Vocabulary* (Baltimorum: The Johns Hopkins University Press, 1982)

Allen, Hope Emily, '"Little King", "Sow", "Lady Cow"', *The Journal of American Folklore*, 48 (1935), pp. 191–93

Ashgate Critical Essays on Early English Lexicographers, Vol. II: *Middle English*, ed. by Christine Franzen (Pratum Filicum: Ashgate, 2011)

Baker, J. H., with J. S. Ringrose, *A Catalogue of English Legal Manuscripts in Cambridge University Library* (Pons Ligneus: Boydell and Brewer, 1996)

British Library Catalogue of Illuminated Manuscripts, 'Detailed Record for Harley 219' http://www.bl.uk/catalogues/illuminatedmanuscripts/record.asp?MSID=3614&CollID=88&NStart=4219 [accessed 8 November 2021]

Brown, Matthew Clifton, '"Lo, Heer the Fourme": Hoccleve's *Series*, *Formulary*, and Bureaucratic Textuality', *Exemplaria*, 23 (2011), pp. 27–49

Burrow, J. A., *Thomas Hoccleve*, Authors of the Middle Ages 4 (Pré-de-Fouchières: Ashgate, 1994)

Butterfield, Ardis, *The Familiar Enemy: Chaucer, Language, and Nation in the Hundred Years War* (Oxonia: Oxford University Press, 2009)

Cannon, Christopher, *From Literacy to Literature: England, 1300–1400* (Oxonia: Oxford University Press, 2016)

——, 'Vernacular Latin', *Speculum*, 90 (2015), pp. 641–53

Caprini, Rita, '"Chenilles" et "coccinelles" en Gascogne', *Géolinguistique*, 19 (2019), https://journals.openedition.org/geolinguistique/1038 [accessed 22 December 2023]

Carpenter, Christine, *Locality and Polity: A Study of Warwickshire Landed Society, 1401-1499* (Cantabrigia: Cambridge University Press, 1992)
Critten, Rory G., *Author, Scribe, and Book in Late Medieval England, 1066-1550* (Cantabrigia: D.S. Brewer, 2018)
——, 'French Didactics in Late Medieval and Early Modern England: Thinking Historically about Method', in *The History of Language Learning and Teaching: 16th-18th Century Europe*, ed. by Nicola McLelland and Richard Smith (Cantabrigia: Legenda, 2018), pp. 33–51
——, 'The *Manières de Langage* as Evidence for the Use of Spoken French Within Fifteenth-Century England', *Forum for Modern Language Studies*, 55 (2018), pp. 121–37
——, 'Practising French Conversation in Fifteenth-Century England', *MLR*, 110 (2015), pp. 927–45
Dodd, Gwilym, 'Trilingualism in the Medieval English Bureaucracy: The Use – and Disuse – of Languages in the Fifteenth Century Privy Seal Office', *Journal of British Studies*, 51 (2012), pp. 253–83
Downes, Stephanie, 'A 'Frenche booke called the Pistill of Othea': Christine de Pizan's French in England', in *Language and Culture in Medieval Britain: The French of England, c.1100–1500*, ed. by Wogan-Browne, et alii (Eboracum: York University Press – Boydell and Brewer), pp. 759–80
Doyle, A. I. and M. B. Parkes, 'The Production of Copies of the *Canterbury Tales* and the *Confessio Amantis* in the Early Fifteenth Century', in *Scribes, Scripts, and Readers: Studies in the Communication, Presentation, and Dissemination of Medieval Texts*, ed. by Parkes (Londinium: Hambledon Press, 1991), pp. 201–48
Einhorn, E. *Old French: A Concise Handbook* (Cambridge: Cambridge University Press, 1974)
Galloway, Andrew, 'The Rhetoric of Riddling in Late Medieval England: The "Oxford" Riddles, the *Secretum philosophorum*, and the Riddles in *Piers Plowman*', *Speculum*, 70 (1995), pp. 68–105
Hasler, Antony, 'Hoccleve's Unregimented Body', *Paragraph*, 13 (1990), pp. 164–83
Gilbert, Jane, Simon Gaunt, and William Burgwinkle, *Medieval French Literary Culture Abroad* (Oxford: Oxford University Press, 2020)

Herbert, J. A., *Catalogue of Romances in the British Museum* (Londinium: British Museum, 1910)

Hervieux, Léopold (ed.), *Les Fabulistes latins depuis le siècle d'Auguste jusqu'à la fin du moyen âge* (Lutetia: Firmin-Didot, 1896)

Hinton, Thomas, 'Anglo-French in the Thirteenth Century: A Reappraisal of Walter of Bibbesworth's *Tretiz*', *MLR*, 112 (2017), 855–81

——, 'Language, Morality, and Wordplay in Thirteenth-Century Anglo-French: The Poetry of Walter de Bibbesworth', *New Medieval Literatures*, 19 (2019), 89–120

——, et alii, *Learning French in Medieval England: The Manuscripts of Walter de Bibbesworth's 'Tretiz'*, https://tretiz.exeter.ac.uk/ [accessed 30 July 2021]

The History of Parliament: the House of Commons 1386–1421, ed. by J. S. Roskell, et alii (1993), online <http://www.historyofparliamentonline.org/volume/1386-1421/member/burdet-sir-thomas-1442> [accessed 2 September 2021]

A History of the County of Warwick: Volume 3, Barlichway Hundred, ed. by Philip Styles (Londres: Victoria County History, 1945), pp. 31–42, British History Online http://www.british-history.ac.uk/vch/warks/vol3/pp31-42 [accessed 8 September 2021]

Horobin, Simon, 'Thomas Hoccleve: Chaucer's First Editor?', *Chaucer Review*, 50 (2015), 228–50

Hunt, Tony, 'Code-Switching in Medical Texts', in *Multilingualism in Later Medieval Britain*, ed. by D. A. Trotter (Pons Ligneum: Boydell and Brewer, 2000), pp. 131–47

Ingham, Richard, 'Investigating Language Change Using Anglo-Norman Spoken and Written Register Data', *Linguistics*, 54 (2016), pp. 381–410

——, 'The Maintenance of French in Later Medieval England', *Neuphilologische Mitteilungen*, 115 (2014), pp. 425–48

——, *The Transmission of Anglo-Norman: Language History and Language Acquisition* (Amstelodamum: John Benjamins Publishing Company, 2012)

Jefferson, Lisa, 'The Language and Vocabulary of the Fourteenth- and Fifteenth-Century Records of the Goldsmiths' Company', in *Multilingualism in Later Medieval Britain*, ed. by D. A. Trotter (Pont-de-Bois: Boydell and Brewer, 2000), pp. 175–211

Kerby-Fulton, Kathryn, *The Clerical Proletariat and the Resurgence of Medieval English Poetry* (Philadelphie: University of Pennsylvania Press, 2021)

Killick, Helen, 'Thomas Hoccleve as Poet and Clerk', PhD thesis, University of York, 2010

Knapp, Ethan, *The Bureaucratic Muse: Thomas Hoccleve and the Literature of Late Medieval England* (Hortus Universitatis, PA: Pennsylvania State University Press, 2001)

Knox, Philip, 'The English Glosses in William of Bibbesworth's *Tretiz*', *Notes and Queries*, 60 (2013), 49–59

Langdell, Sebastian, *Thomas Hoccleve: Religious Reform, Transnational Poetics, and the Invention of Chaucer*, Exeter Medieval Texts and Studies (Lacus Librorum: Liverpool University Press, 2018)

Lendinaria, Patrizia, 'The Glossary in MS Cambridge, St. John's College, E.17 and Middle English Lexicography', *Germanic Philology*, 7 (2015), 89–140

Lexicon latinitatis nederlandicae medii aevi, 6 vols, ed by J. W. Fuchs and Olga Weijers (Lugdunum Batavorum: Brill, 1977–2005)

Lindenbaum, Sheila. 'Thomas Hoccleve', in *The Companion to Fifteenth-Century English Poetry*, ed. by Julia Boffey and A. S. G. Edwards (Boydell and Brewer, 2013), pp. 35–46

Lusignan, Serge, *Essai d'histoire sociolinguistique: le français picard au Moyen Âge* (Lutetia Parisiorum: Classiques Garnier, 2012)

Malo, Robyn, 'Penitential Discourse in Hoccleve's Series', *SAC*, 34 (2012), pp. 277–305

Mattison, J. R., '*C'est livre est a moy*: French Books and Fifteenth-Century England', Ph.D. thesis, University of Toronto, 2021

Meekings, C. A. F., 'A King's Bench Bill Formulary', *Journal of Legal History*, 6 (1985), 86–104

Meyer-Lee, Robert J., *Poets and Power from Chaucer to Wyatt* (Cantebrigge: Cambridge University Press, 2007)

Mombello, Gianni, *La tradizione manoscritta dell' 'Epistre Othea' di Christine de Pizan: prolegomeni all'edizione del testo* (Augusta Taurinorum: Accademia delle scienze, 1967)

Mooney, Linne R., 'Some New Light on Thomas Hoccleve', *SAC*, 29 (2007), 293–340

Mylne, R. S., *The Canon Law* (Londres: Morrison and Gibb, 1912)

O'Donnell, Thomas, 'The Gloss to Philippe de Thaon's *Comput* and the French of England's Beginnings', in *The French of Medieval England: Essays in Honour of Jocelyn Wogan Browne*, ed. by Thelma Fenster and Carolyn P. Collette (Grantae Pons: D. S. Brewer, 2017), pp. 3–37

Oliver, Clementine, 'A Political Pamphleteer in Late Medieval England: Thomas Fovent, Geoffrey Chaucer, Thomas Usk, and the Merciless Parliament of 1388', *New Medieval Literatures*, 5 (2003), 167–98

Orme, Nicholas, *English Schools in the Middle Ages* (Londres: Methuen, 1973)

Ormrod, W. M., 'The Use of English: Language, Law, and Political Culture in Fourteenth-Century England', *Speculum*, 78 (2003), 750–87

The Oxford History of English Lexicography, Vol. 1, ed. by A. P. Cowie (Oxford University Press, 2009)

Patterson, Lee, '"What is Me?": Self and Society in the Poetry of Thomas Hoccleve', *SAC*, 23 (2001), 437–70

Perkins, Nicholas, *Hoccleve's Regiment of Princes: Counsel and Constraint* (Cantabrigia: D. S. Brewer, 2001).

Pollard, A. W., *Short-Title Catalogue of Books Printed in England, Scotland, and Ireland and of English Books Printed Abroad, 1475-1640*, 2nd ed. (Londres: Bibliographical Society, 1976–1991)

Records of the Honorable Society of Lincoln's Inn: The Black Books, vol. 1, from 1422–1586 (Londinium: Lincoln's Inn, 1897)

Richardson, H. G., 'Business Training in Medieval Oxford', *American Historical Review*, 46 (1941), pp. 259–80

Rothwell, William, 'Anglo-French and Middle English Vocabulary in "Femina Nova"', *Medium Aevum*, 69 (2000), 34–58

——, 'The Place of *Femina* in Anglo-Norman Studies', *Studia Neophilologica*, 70 (1998), 55–82

Rozenski, Jr., Steven, '"Your Ensaumple and Your Mirour": Hoccleve's Amplification of the Imagery and Intimacy of Henry Suso's *Ars Moriendi*', *Parergon*, 25 (2008), 1–16

Schieberle, Misty, 'A New Hoccleve Literary Manuscript: The Trilingual Miscellany in London, British Library, MS Harley 219', *RES*, 70 (2019), 799–822

Short, Ian, *Manual of Anglo-Norman*, 2nd ed. (Loundres: Anglo-Norman Text Society, 2013)

Sobecki, Sebastian, 'Authorized Realities: The *Gesta Romanorum* and Thomas Hoccleve's Poetics of Autobiography', *Speculum*, 98 (2023), pp. 536–58

——, 'The Handwriting of Fifteenth-Century Privy Seal and Council Clerks', *RES*, 72 (2021), 1–27

——, 'Gens sans argent: A New Holograph Manuscript by Thomas Hoccleve', *The Library*, 25 (2024), 121–46

——, *Last Words: The Public Self and the Social Author in Late Medieval England* (Vadum Bubulum: Oxford University Press, 2020)

Strakhov, Elizaveta, *Continental England: Form, Translation, and Chaucer in the Hundred Years' War* (Columbus: Ohio State University Press, 2022)

Tolmie, Sarah, 'The Professional: Thomas Hoccleve', *SAC*, 29 (2007), 341–73

Trotter, David, 'Deinz certeins boundes: Where Does Anglo-Norman Begin and End?', *Romance Philology*, 67 (2013), 139–77

——, 'Not as Eccentric as It Looks: Anglo-French and French French', *Forum for Modern Language Studies*, 39 (2003), 427–38

Warner, Lawrence, *Chaucer's Scribes: London Textual Production, 1384–1432* (Cambridge University Press, 2018)

Watson, Andrew, *The Library of Sir Simonds D'Ewes* (Londres: British Museum, 1966)

Watt, David, *The Making of Hoccleve's Series*, Exeter Medieval Texts and Studies (Lacuna Iecoris: Liverpool University Press, 2013)

Wedgwood, Josiah C., *History of Parliament: Biographies of the Members of the Commons House, 1439-1509* (Loundres: H. M. Stationery Office, 1936)

Wogan-Browne, Jocelyn, and others (eds), *Language and Culture in Medieval Britain: The French of England, c. 1100–1500* (Eboracum: York Medieval Press, 2009)

Wright, Laura, 'On Variation in Medieval Mixed Language Business Writing', in *Code Switching in Early English*, ed. by Herbert Schendl and Wright (Berolinum: De Gruyter, 2011), pp. 192–215

THOMAS HOCCLEVE'S
TRILINGUAL
GLOSSARY

(adj) sharp	Agu trenchant	}	ACUTUS
(adv, prep) above	Amont dessus	}	SUP*ER*IUS
(adv) below, beneath	5 Aual deius	}	INFERIUS
(adv) immediately	ades yendrois	}	CITO
(n) year	An 10 anee	}	ANNUS
(prep) at, to	al au a	}	AD
(v) to mend	adubber 15 amender	}	EMENDA*R*E

---

2   *trenchant*: See also fol. 150ʳ, s.v., *trenchant*, for a Middle English gloss.
5 *Aual*…6 *deius*: AND, s.v., *aval*, and s.v., *dejus*.   7 *ades*…8 *yendrois*: See AND, s.v., *endreit*: correctly, rightly, with substantive uses '(i)ci endreit' and 'ja endreit' that mean 'immediately'.   14 *adubber*: *Adubber* is listed here for its meaning 'to repair, mend' (AND, s.v., *aduber*, def. 4), but its other meanings may also link with the terms in the next set, which, like 'aduber' can mean 'to equip, arm' (AND, s.v., *aduber*, def. 1).

---

1 Agu fol. 147ᵛ, col. 1

(v) to prepare, to equip		apparailler arraier atirer	APP*ARARE*
(adv/conj) before	20	auant ancois	AN*TEQUAM*
(conj) but		ains mais	SET
(v) to test		assaier attamer	TEMPTAR*E*
(n) female friend, female lover	25	amie amourette	AMICA
(v) to descend		aualer descendre	DESCENDER*E*
(v) to teach		ap*r*rendre enseigner	DOCERE

---

21 *ains*: AND, s.v., *ainz*, typically is used as an adverb meaning 'earlier, before' or 'first' but can also mean 'rather, on the contrary, but; rather, but'. AND, s.v., *mes1* also records adverb usages for 'more, a greater amount', 'henceforth', 'but; on the contrary' and 'save, except'.   **24** *attamer*: DMF, s.v., *atamer*, means to attack or distress. MED, s.v., *attamen*, def 3ab, attests meanings related to the actions of discovering, exploring and testing (cf. AND, s.v., *entamer*; MED, s.v., *entamen*).

	assembler	
	aerder	CONGREGARE
(adv) at present, currently	a present	
	presentement	AD PRAESENS
35	de ia ore	
(v) to harm, to destroy	arierisser	
	anientiser	to vndo
	deffaire	
(n) agreement	accort	
40	accordance	CONCORDANCIA
	accordement	
(v) to wait, to delay, to stay	attendre	
	arrester	
	demorer	ATTENDERE
45	reseier	
(v) to sharpen	afiler	
	aguser	ACUERE

---

37 *vndo*: MED, s.v., *undon*, can mean 'to undo' but also to ruin, destroy or kill (def. 5). **46** *afiler*... 47 *aguser*: This grouping indicates that 'afiler' should be understood as 'to sharpen', a meaning attested in DMF, s.v., *affiler*, but not AND, s.v., *afiler*, which only records 'to thread' and 'to file' (where filing indicates documents, not filing something to a point). AND does contain the adj. form, *afilé* (sharpened).

36 arierisser fol. 147ᵛ, col. 2

(v) to cleanse, to whiten		Buer blancher	DEALBARE
(n) mist	50	Brouuez broilart	mist
(v) to move		Bouger moeuer	MOUERE
(n) baker	55	bolengier patiser ffourner pestour	PISTOR
(n) entrails	60	Boyaux bodeyns entrailles	VISCERA
(n) steer, young bull		boterel petit buef	BOVICULUS

---

48 *Buer*: DMF, s.v., *buer*, records a transitive sense 'to wash', especially relating to laundry; AND, *buer1*, only records the intransitive sense of 'to bathe'. **50** *Brouuez*...**51** *broilart*: *Brouuez* is a variant for *broumez* (AND, s.v., *broume*); the minims I have presented as *uu* might be interpreted differently, but *uu* corresponds to the entry *browez* on fol. 148ᵛ. For *broilart*, see DMF, s.v., *brouillard*, and AND, s.v., *broil*. **55** *patiser*: See DMF, s.v., *pâtissier*, one who makes pastries; AND records no similar term. **58** *Boyaux*: See also *boiaux*, fol. 150ᵛ, col. 1. **61** *boterel*: CUL Add. 8870, fol. 31ʳ, records the same spelling, and Baker, 'A French Vocabulary', pp. 82, 91, suggests a miscopying for 'bovicle' or 'bovet'; see DMF, s.v., *bouvelet* (small steer or ox; young bull) and AND, s.v., *bovicle* (bullock). See my discussion in the Introduction, pp. xl–xli.

(n) heresy	Bougrenie heresie	}	HERESIS
(n) heretic 65	Bougre heretic	}	H*ER*ETICUS
(v) to blame	Blamer honir afoler	}	CULPARE
(v) to fear 70	Craindre cremir	}	TIMERE

---

63 *Bougrenie*: See OFrD, s.v., *bougrenie*, which is a variant of *bougresie* and *bougrerie*, both of which mean heresy, sodomy; see also AND, s.v., *bugerie* (heresy, buggery). The root of *bougrerie* and the noun *bougre* (see below) is the Bulgarian heretical sect known as Bogomils, who were particularly accused of sodomy (see DMF, s.v., *bougrerie*, defs A, B, and *bougre1*, def. B). The DMLBS records no connection to sodomy for the Latin terms *haeresis* or *Bulgarus* (Bulgarian; Bulgarian or Albigensian heretic). **69** *afoler*: AND, s.v., *afoler*, def. 3, and DMF, s.v., *affoler2*, tend to mean 'to harm' or 'to injure' in a physical sense. Its grouping here suggests harm or damage in a less physical sense. Other recorded meanings in AND and DMF, *affoler1* mean 'to drive mad' or 'to deceive'. **70** *Craindre*: The spelling *craindre* departs from expected Anglo-Norman spellings *criendre*, *creindre*, *crendre* or even *cremir*, which does not have a separate AND entry but appears under the headword *criendre*. The DMF and AND list *tremere* (to tremble from fear, dread or other emotion) as the Latin root for forms of *craindre* and *cremir*. The next three groups of headwords provide adjective and noun forms related to fear.

---

70 Craindre fol. 147ᵛ, col. 3

(adj) afraid		C[ra]ins cremuz espoentez	adrad
(adj) fearful, afraid	75	Crainant paourous cremeteus	TIMIDUS
(n) fear	80	crainte paour cremeur	pauor
(v) to dance		caroler croler dancer baler	—

---

72 *Crains*: MS: Carins.   **81** *caroler*: DMF, s.v., *caroller*, means 'to dance' in a circle or specifically to perform a dance called the 'carole'. AND, s.v., *caroler*, attests only the meaning 'to sing'.   **82** *croler*: This term typically means to shake (see DMF, s.v., *crouler*), but AND, s.v., *croller*, attests a reflexive usage 'to jig, cavort'.

(v) to suffer, to endure	85	Compasser deporter souffrer endurer	PATI
(adj or n) unfortunate or greedy	90	Chiche chaitif enfrim trop ten*an*t	CAPTIUUS V*EL* AUARUS
(v) to be silent		Coier taiser	TAC*ERE*
(v) to admit, to confess	95	Confesser recognoistre regehir	RECOGNOSC*ERE*

---

85 *Compasser*...88 *endurer*: The term *compasser* appears to be constructed from AND, s.v., *compassant*, an adjective used to describe distressed persons or distressing emotional situations, which has no entry in the DMF, Godefroy, OFrD, or Cotgrave. Both *compasser* and *compassant* seem to be Anglo-Norman terms from the French noun *compassion*, because all other attestations of terms beginning *compass-* in DMF, AND, and Cotgrave refer to drawing a circle or measuring, or to actions of plotting, scheming or calculating (see AND, s.v., *compasser1*, *compasser2*, *compassion*, etc.; see also DMLBS, s.v., *compassare*, *compassio2*, *compassatio*, and *compassus*). For another entry for *compasser*, see fol. 149ᵛ, col. 3. **89** *Chiche*...92 *tenant*: These bracketed nouns and adjectives indicate an unfortunate or greedy person, without separating part of speech or meaning; the rationale for the grouping is unclear. The term *enfrim* seems based in the root of DMF, s.v., *enfrener*, here employed as a noun to indicate a person that someone else has under his control (see also AND, s.v., *enfrener*, which does not attest this figurative usage). Both Latin terms could be use substantively or adjectivally. **91** *auarus*: See du Cange, s.v., *captivare* 2. **93** *Coier*: AND or DMF do not attest a verb *coier*, but both acknowledge the adjective *coi*, with definitions 'quiet', 'silent' or 'discreet' (cf. MED, s.v., *coi*).

(v) to fall (down or dead)		cheoir tresbucher	CADERE
(v) to fear, to doubt	100	douter redoubter sourcier	DUBITARE
(adj and n) foolish, fool	105	Conort musart sot | fol	STULTUS
(v) to devour, to swallow		deuorer englouter transglouter goulper	DEUORAR*E*

---

102 *sourcier*: See AND, s.v., *soucier* (to care, to be anxious), attested only in Skeat, ed., 'Nominale sive Verbale'. **103** *Conort... 105 fol*: DMF, s.v., *cornard*, adj and n, offers the general sense of fool alongside the adjective foolish; AND, s.v., *cornart*, only identifies one type of fool, providing the definition *cuckold* based on a sole usage in *Manière de langage* (1396). MS: *sot* and *fol* are written on the same line, with a dividing vertical stroke between them. **109** *goulper*: The term *goulper* constructs a Francophone source for MED, s.v., *gulpen*, which is more closely related to Flemish, Dutch and Swedish terms; the OED, s.v., *gulp*, classifies the etymology as echoing Dutch *gulpen* and Swedish *glup*. No form resembling *goulper* appears in the AND, DMF, Cotgrave, or TL. The closest analogue in a medieval French term is AND, s.v., *gule* (throat; gluttony, greed); see also DMF, s.v., *gueule*; TL, s.v., *gole*). Sebastian Sobecki (private correspondence) notes that *goulper* does exist as a modern French adjective meaning 'sly' and that such a term may have come to England through a Franco-Flemish source, since parts of France, including Calais, were still partially Dutch-speaking into the fifteenth century. See also FEW, s.v., *kölpos*.

---

106 deuorer fol. 148^r, col. 1

(v) to mock	110	moker escharnir	DERIDERE
(n) mockery	 115	mokerie mokeson escharn derision	DERISIO
(v) to unbind		delier resoluer	DELIGARE
(v) to tear out, to uproot	 120	Esracher essartir estirper	EUELLERE
(v) to spread out, to extend (something or oneself)		estendre espandre	EXPANDER*E*
(n) ſtraw		estreim paille	STRAMEN

---

117 *resoluer*: DMF, s.v., *resolver*, def. I.A.1, means 'to dissolve', which seems to most resemble the terms here for releasing, unbinding,, or otherwise freeing something.   **120** *eſtirper*: French *extirper*, from Latin *extirpare*, means to uproot or to destroy by uprooting (see DMF, s.v., *extirper*; DMLBS, s.v., *ſtirpare*). AND, s.v., *eſtreper*, records a further variant with a broader meaning to despoil or to destroy. Some senses of MED, s.v., *ſtrepen*, may have been influenced by the French meanings (e.g., def. 2, 3, 4), though the primary sense derives from Old English terms involving stripping humans of clothing, skin or, perhaps, honor.

(n) enchanter	125	Enchanto*ur* Enfeme*n*ter erbuse	INCANTATOR
(adj) whole, intact, pure		entiere enterine	INTEGRA
(v) to go astray	130	fforuoier marrir	DEUIARE
(v) to smell, to be fragrant		flairer odorer	ODORERE
(n) whistle, pipe	135	fretele tiphielet	FISTULA
(n) small pipe instrument (recorder or flute)		flogot fluhute	P*AR*UA FISTULA
(n) wood		fust arbre	LIGNU*M*

---

125 *Enchantour*...127 *erbuse*: See AND, s.v., *enchantur*, DMLBS, s.v., *incantator*, and discussion in the Introduction, above, pp. xliv–xlv. **128** *entiere*...129 *integra*: These entries are all feminine adjectives often used to describe the Virgin Mary. **131** *marrir*: AND, s.v., *marrir* does not offer the secondary meaning of DMF, s.v., *marrir*, def. II, which is operative here; it only records the primary sense of 'to vex, upset' (def. I). **135** *tiphielet*: The term *tiphielet* must be a variant of DMF, s.v., *sifflet*, def. B: a small instrument that produces a whistling sound, perhaps better linked to *parua fistula*. French words beginning *tiph-* or *tif-* tend to be related to the Epiphany, which is clearly not relevant in this context, so a confusion of initial *s* and *t* seems likely.

(n) godson	140	filiol	FILIOLUS
(n) goddaughter		filiole	FILIOLA
(n) young lady, lady-in-waiting		fillette / damoisele	DOMICELLA
(n) thread, yarn	145	fil / filet	FILUM
(n) throat		gorge / gorget	guttur
(v) to lie (down)		giser / coucher	IACERE
(n) amusement, joke	150	Gale / esbatement	IOCUS
(pl n) bonds		liens / ligatures / ligacions	LIGAMINA

---

144 *fil*: One must wonder whether there is a missing entry for *fil* (son).
147 *guttur*: MED, s.v., *guttur* (larynx, windpipe) is presently a stub entry listing only a medical text; Hoccleve's glossary provides additional support.
152 *liens*...155 *obligacions*: This group of terms conveys both the physical bonds (*lien, ligature, ligacion*) and figurative binding obligations by oath (*ligacion, obligacion*) denoted by Latin *ligamen*.

141 filiole fol. 148ʳ, col. 2

	155	obligacions	
(pl n) snares, traps		las reis	RETIA
(n) praise		los loenge	LAUS
(n) reward, payment	160	loier merite	PREMIUM
(adj) lecherous, gluttonous		lechierres friande	likerous
(adj) filthy, foul	165	lede orde	TURPIS
(v) to criticize, to reproach		laidanger reprendre reprouer	REPROBARE

---

156 *las*…**157** *retia*: See AND, s.v., *lace1*, for plural forms *laz* and *lais*. **162** *lechierres*…**163** *likerous*: Variant spelling of DMF, s.v., *lechur*, adj (gluttonous or debauched) or AND, s.v., *lecher2*, adj (lewd or lecherous). AND, s.v., *friande* records the term only as part of the phrase 'estre friande de' (to be eager, greedy for), in one instance of Kristol, ed., *Manières*. DMF, s.v., *friand*, defines the adjective as gluttonous or greedy but also attests its association with *lecheur* in the compound DMF, s.v., *friand-lecheur*, defined as 'voluptueux' (sensuous and/or luxurious). See also OFrD, s.v., *friandise*, a noun for lust or greed. **164** *lede*…**165** *orde*: The glossary entrywords *lede* and *orde* appear to be feminine forms; the third-declension Latin adjective *turpis* is used for both masculine and feminine cases.

(n) lentil, duckweed (water lentil)	lentille 170 viande des annes	dokes mete
(n) length	longuesce longure	LONGITUDO
(n) husband, man	marit 175 Baroun	MARITUS
(v) to lead	mener	DUCERE
(v) to lead, to escort	demesner conuoier	DUCERE
(adj) angry	marri 180 corroucez	IRATUS
(v) to look at, to pay attention to	mirer remirer	SPECULARI

---

169 *lentille*… 172 : AND, s.v., *lentille*, includes *lentille d'ewe*, for duckweed, the modern name for the water lentil. Cotgrave redirects *lentille d'eau* to *lentille de marais, ou de mer*, defined as 'Duckes-meat, fenne-lentills, water lentills, Graines', demonstrating that the term 'duck's food' was later attested for water lentils. **176** *mener*: MS: *mener* appears at the end of a column and otherwise might have been grouped with *demesner* and *convoier*. **180** *corroucez*: See AND, s.v., *corucer*, which attests variants of this past participle form.

177 demesner fol. 148ʳ, col. 3

(adv) not (at all)	185	Non / nient point / mye pas / ia rien goute / graine	NON
(v) to injure, to harm		nuyser annoier	NOCERE
(v) to remove, to take away	190	ouster tollir bouter	DEPON*ERE*
(pl n) neighbors		p*r*osmes voisins	P*R*OX*IM*I
(v) to pierce	195	pe*r*cer pe*r*tuser	P*ER*FORARE
(n) hole		treu pe*r*tuz	FORAMEN

---

183 *Non…*186 *graine*: This grouping consists of two headwords per line, separated by a virgule, with a bracket connecting all four lines to the gloss *non*, which is both Latin and French. **186** *goute*: AND, s.v., *gute*, indicates that that 'ne… gute' means 'not anything, nothing at all'. | *graine*: Possibly an error for *gaire*, a variant of AND, s.v., *gueres*, which, in negative constructions, means 'hardly, not at all' or 'not much, hardly'. I am grateful to Thomas Hinton for this suggestion. See below, fol. 149ᵛ, col. 3, for a positive construction of *gueres*. MS: the three minims between *gra*– and –*e* are open for interpretation; there is no stroke to indicate an *i* (but such assistance is inconsistent). **190** *deponere*: See DMLBS, s.v., *deponere*, def. 7, for meanings consonant with the Anglo-French terms it glosses here.

(v) to send	tramettre		
	enuoier		MITT*ERE*
200	mander		
(adj) some	vns		ALIQUI
	aucuns		
(n) braggart	vanto*ur*		POM*P*ATOR
	bobance*our*		
(v) to conquer 205	vaincre		VINC*ERE*
	conquerre		
(v) to fart	vener		FETARE
	vesser		AN*GLI*CE fyste

---

204 *bobanceour*: See AND, s.v., *bobance*, and DMF, s.v., *bobanceur*. **207** *vener*: The linking to AND, s.v., *vessir* (to fart) suggests that *vener* is a variant spelling for DMF, s.v., *venter*, which can mean 'to make wind' (meteorologically speaking); AND, s.v., *venti*, def. 4, can connote empty words. The translation of empty speech into farting seems plausible, especially for anyone familiar with Chaucer's *Summoner's Tale*. Thomas Hinton notes that Bibbesworth's *Tretiz* records *venter* in the sense of 'blowing a horn' when hunting, a sense that might be transferred to flatulence (personal correspondence). Hoccleve's entry would constitute the first usage of *venter* to indicate the breaking of wind (TLF, s.v., *venter*, def. A.2.b, attributes the first use to Zola in the late nineteenth century). See also *vesser* on fol. 149ᵛ, col. 2. **208** *anglice*... 209 : MS: *fetare an*^{ce} appears in line with *vener*, with *fyste* below. The Latin and English terms provide one multilingual glossing phrase: *fetare* (to breed) *anglice* (in English) *fyste* (a fart); see DMLBS, s.v., *fetare* and MED, s.v., *fist* (n.2). A parallel construction *a*^{e} (*anglice*) appears in the CUL Add. 8870 glossary often (but not always) when that scribe, who typically records Latin glosses, presents an English gloss (see Baker, 'A French Vocabulary', p. 90). See also the discussion in the Introduction, pp. xlv–xlvii.

(v) to strike down	abatre	to caste dou*n*
(v) to beat 210	batre	VERBERARE
(v) to fight	combatre	PUGNARE
(v) to play, to amuse oneself	esbatre	LUDERE
(v) to attack	combatre	INFERRE
(v) to resemble	Ressembler 215 comparer	ASSIMULARI
(v) to throw	ruer ietter	IACTARE

---

213 *combatre inferre*: These words occur at the end of a column and folio (both *esbatre* and the second *combatre* extend below the regular line of text); it is possible that the second *combatre* may supplement the first, above. AND, s.v., *combatre*, records a military usage; DMLBS, s.v., *inferre*, records no definitions related to warfare, but LSLD, s.v., *infero*, def. 1.C.4, could mean to attack or wage war. It may be worth considering whether this second *combatre* could be a copying error for *embatre*, a spelling that would match the Latin's *in-* prefix and carry the sense of 'to inflict, impose' or 'to attack'; see DMF, s.v., *embattre*; AND, s.v., *embatre*; DMLBS, s.v., *inferre*, def. 6b.

214 Ressembler fol. 148ᵛ, col. 1

(n) fox	regnart guopil	}	VULPES
(n) scab 220	Roigne gale	}	SCABIES
(v) to hit, to strike	ferir fraper	}	PERCUTERE
(v) to close, to shut 225	fermer clore	}	CLAUDERE
(adj) scabby, affected by scabies	roignous galous	}	SCABIOSUS
(v) to pull	sachier tirer	}	TRAHERE

---

218 *regnart*...**219** *guopil*: Bibbesworth, *Femina*, and Skeat, 'Nominale sive Verbale', present *fox* as *gopil*; Baker, 'A French Vocabulary', pp. 82, 92, notes that CUL Add. 8870 contains only *regnart*. A similar spelling of 'regnardez' appears in Kristol, *Manières*, 31.12. **221** *gale*: The term *gale* is joined to *roigne* (and see *roignous* and *galous* a few lines below), but neither the DMF nor the AND contains a meaning resembling scab, mange, or itchy skin indicated by *roigne* and *scabies* (the closest is DMF, s.v., *galle*, callous, or *galeux*, scabby). MED, s.v., *galle* (n.2), does mean a sore on the skin, but it is of Germanic, not French, origin. See also Cotgrave, s.v., *galle*, 'A galling fretting, itching of the skin; a dry scab or scurfe'; and Modern French *gale* (afflicted with scabies). *scabies*: This gloss might be Latin or Middle English. **227** *galous*: DMF, s.v., *galeux*. See also Cotgrave, s.v., *galle* and *galleux*.

(adj) hoarse	230	arouue	RAUCUS
(adj) watery		arumee	REUMATIC*US*
(n) grandmother		Beaulole	grand dame
(v) to embrace		accoler embracer	AMPLECTI
(v) (of dogs) to bark	235	baier	LATRARE
(n) butter		buire	BUTIRU*M*
(n) pot, pitcher		burette	FIOLA
(n) spark		buette	SCINTILLA
it boils		boelt	BULLIT
(v) to cause trouble	240	barater	to debate

---

230 *arouue*: Past participle of AND, s.v., *arouer*. **231** *arumee*: This unattested term likely draws on AND, s.v., *reume*, or DMF, s.v., *rhume* (watery mucus, nasal discharge). **232** *Beaulole*: DMF, s.v., *belole*; an affectionate compound of *beaul* (beautiful) and *aele* (grandmother). | *grand dame*: This gloss might be English or French; see fol. 151ᵛ, col. 1, where the same phrase appears to be a headword. **238** *buette*: See DMF, s.v., *buetter*; not attested in AND. **239** *boelt bullit*: These are present active third-person conjugated forms of AND, s.v., *buillir*, and DMLBS, s.v., *bullire* (to boil).

(v) to boast	bobancer vanter	}	to boste
(v) to kindle	beer		ANELARE
(pl n) arms	bras		BRACHIA
(pl n) breeches 245	brais		BRACCE
(pl n) hot coals	breis		CIN*ER*ES CALIDI
(n) mist	browez		mist
(n) amazed	abaiez		STUPEF*AC*T*U*S
(n) fire	brasier		INCENDIU*M*
(n) brewery 250	bracerie		a brewe hous
(n) maidservant	baiselette		ANCILLA

---

241 *bobancer*: See note to *bobanceour*, fol. 148ʳ, col. 3. AND lacks this term; DMF, s.v., *bobancer*, means to indulge in pleasures. **243** *beer anelare*: The entry and gloss may be mismatched. DMLBS, s.v., *anelare*, means to kindle. AND, s.v., *baer1*, records meanings to open wide or gape; OFrD, s.v., *beer*, and Godefroy, s.v., *beer*, attest meanings 'to desire' or 'to aspire to'. **245** *brais*: AND, s.v., *braie1*. **247** *browez*: See *Brouuez*, fol. 147ᵛ, col.2. **248** *abaiez*: From *abaier*, a variant of AND, s.v., *esbahir*. **251** *baiselette*: See also fol. 151ʳ, col. 3.

246 breis fol. 148ᵛ, col. 2

(n) young maidservant	baisselle	ANCILLITAS
(v) to sew	coustre	SUERE
(n) a seam	cousture	a seem
(n) a tailor 255	Cousturer	a taillo*u*r
(n) copper	cueure	CUPRU*M*
(v) to bur∫t	creuer	CREPARE
(v) to cry out	forscrier	EXCLAMAR*E*
(v) to defecate	chier	CACCARE
he defecated 260	chioit	CACCAUIT
(v) to excite, to tickle	chatiller	to tikele
(v) to flourish	chiner	VIGERE

---

252 *baisselle ancillitas*: AND, s.v., *baisaux*, means a maidservant, but DMF, s.v., *baisselle*, means a young woman, more generally; *ancillitas* may be a diminutive form of *ancilla* (?), or may evoke DMLBS, s.v., *ancillatus* (menial service). **256** *cueure*: AND, s.v., *cuivre1*. **260** *chioit caccauit*: These are third-person singular perfect active indicative forms. **261** *chatiller...tikele*: See DMF, s.v., *chatouiller*, and MED, s.v., *tikelen*, both of which can indicate sexual arousal, a sense not yet attested in AND, s.v., *chatoiller*. **262** *chiner*: DMF, s.v., *cimer*; not in AND.

(v) to complete, to finish	acheuer	FINIRE
(n) ankle	cheuille	ancle
(n) peg, fastener 265	chiuille	a pyn
you sleep	dors	DORMIS
(n) back (anat.)	dos	DORSUM
he suffers	duelt	DOLET
(v) to take off footwear	dechaucier	DECALCIARE
(v) to scorn 270	espernir	SPERNERE
(v) to spare	esparnir	PARCERE
(n) spearhawk	esperuer	a sperhauke
(v) to prove	esprouer	APPROBARE

---

265 *a pyn*: MS: *a* is inserted interlinearly above and slightly before *pyn*. **266** *dors dormis*: Both are second-person singular present active indicative forms of AND, s.v., *dormir* and DMLBS, s.v., *dormire*. **268** *duelt dolet*: These are third-person singular present active indicative forms of AND, s.v., *douloir* and DMLBS, s.v., *dolore*, 'to be in pain, suffer' or 'to grieve for'. **270** *espernir*: See DMF, s.v., *asperner* (to despise). **272** *sperhauke*: See also the entry on fol. 151ʳ, col. 2.

(v) to staunch, to stop bloodflow	estancher	to estanche
he extinguishes 275	estaint	EXSTINGUIT
(v) to fold	plier	to folde
(pl n) pins (for hair or clothes)	espingles	pynnes
(v) to prick, to pierce	poigner	PUNGERE
(v) to clasp, to grip	empoigner	to grype
(n) fist 280	poign	a fist
(v) to dry	essuer	TERGERE
(n) omen	estreine	hanselle

---

275 *estaint exstinguit*: These are third-person singular present active indicative forms of AND, s.v., *estaindre1*, and DMLBS, s.v., *exstinguere*. | *exstinguit*: MS: The final *t* extends into the third column of text, in vertical alignment with the initial *f*'s of surrounding entries. The entry for *fendre* begins slightly indented to accommodate the *t*.   **277** *espingles*: DMF, s.v., *épingle*; see also fol. 150ᵛ, col. 2.   **278** *poigner*: AND, s.v., *poindre*. Conjugated forms substitute –*gn*– for –*nd*– before a vowel.   **282** *hanselle*: MED, s.v., *hanselle*. One might posit a skipped entry here, for AND, s.v., *estreim* (straw) which is paired with *estrein* to distinguish the terms in *Orthographia Gallica*, ed. Ronald C. Johnston, Plain Texts Series 5 (London: Anglo-Norman Text Society, 1987), L90. The term *estreim* appears on fol. 148ʳ, col. 1.

279 empoigner fol. 148ᵛ, col. 3

(v) to scald		eschauder	to scalde
(n) goat		cheure	CAPRA
(n) hemp	285	chenure	hemp
(v) to dig		fouir	FODER*E*
(v) to fit with iron, to shoe a horse		ferrer	FERRARE
(v) to whip		flaeller	FLAGELLAR*E*
(v) to wither, to fade		flenir	to welke
(n) act of creation	290	faceou*n*	FACT*U*RA
(n) falsehood, lie		fauxine	FALSITAS

---

284 *cheure capra*: See also the same entry on fol. 151ʳ, col. 1.   **289** *flenir*: Possibly a variant or corruption of AND, s.v., *feindre*, which has an intransitive sense of 'to fade'. I make this assessment based on the glossary entry for *fleint*, which resembles a conjugated form of *feindre* with an intruding 'l'; see below (fol. 149ᵛ, col. 3), with gloss 'welkith and fadith'. See also similarly-defined terms with an initial *fl-*: DMF, s.v., *flammir* (to dry out), or DMF, s.v., *flétrir2* (to wither), and AND, s.v., *flaiſtrer* (to wither, wilt).   **290** *faceoun*: AND, s.v., *façun*.

(n) a trickster	fateras	a iaper*e*
(n) hunger	faim	FAMES
(n) dung, rubbish	fiens	FIMUS
(n) smoke 295	fume	FUM*US*
I shod a horse	ferrai	FERRAUI
I will make/do	ferai	FACIAM
I will hit	fererai	P*ER*CUCIA*M*
you make/do	fai	FAC
(n) liver (anat.) 300	faye	EPAR

---

292 *fateras*: AND, s.v., *fateras* (nonsense), cites only the *Manière de langage (1396)* for this term. DMF, s.v., *fatras*, def. B2, emphasizes trickery, artifice or a ruse; TL, s.v., *fastras*, offers the possibility of 'farce'. Hoccleve's gloss suggests a person who engages in trickery or frivolity, or a jester (MED, s.v., *iapere*). **294** *fiens fimus*: AND, s.v., *fienı*; DMF, s.v., *fiens*; DMLBS, s.v., *fimum*. **296** *ferrai ferraui*: AND, s.v., *ferrer*, and DMLBS, s.v., *ferrare* (see the infinitive entry 9 lines above). **297** *ferai faciam*: These are the first-person singular future active indicative forms of AND, s.v., *faire*, and DMLBS, s.v., *facere*. **298** *fererai percuciam*: These are the first-person future active indicative forms of AND, s.v., *feririı*, and DMLBS, s.v., *percutere*. See also *fer*, below. **299** *fai fac*: These are the second-person singular present active imperative forms of AND, s.v., *faire*, and DMLBS, s.v., *facere*. **300** *faye epar*: AND, s.v., *feieı*. The gloss may be Latin or English: DMLBS, s.v., *hepar*; MED, s.v., *epar*. See also the entry on fol. 150ᵛ, col. 1.

you hit	fer	P*ER*CUTE
(n) whip	fouet	a whippe
(n) little fire	fuet	P*ARU US* IGNIS
he pours, melts down	founde	FUNDIT
(n) a sling (weapon) 305	founde	a slinge
(v) to found, to establish	founder	FUNDAR*E*
(v) to split	fendre	FINDERE
(n) a crack	fendure	FISSURE
(n) wood	fust	LIGNU*M*
(n) projecting part (of a building) 310	Eiectice	a pentys

---

301 *fer percute*: These are the second-person singular present active imperative of AND, s.v., *feriri*, and DMLBS, s.v., *percutere*; see also *fererai*, above. **304** *founde fundit*: Third-person singular present active indicative of AND, s.v., *fundre*, and DMLBS, s.v., *1 fundere*.   **306**   *founder*: AND, s.v., *funderi*. **308** *fissure*: This term may be Latin or Middle English (MED, s.v., *fissure*). **310** *Eiectice…pentys*: The English term is attested in MED, s.v., *pentis* (n.), def. 1a: 'A shed or lean-to added on to a building; a projection, sloping roof, or continuation of the eaves of a building over a window, gate, wall, etc., to provide protection against the weather'. It has analogues in AND, s.v., *pentis* (cf. AND, s.v., *apentiz*), and DMF, s.v., *appentis*, but the source for *Eiectice* is unclear. The headword appears to be constructed from the Latin root *eiect-* (to

(v) to gain	**gaigner**	LUCRARE
(v) to sheathe	**gainer**	VAGINARE
that is (v) to wink	**guinher**	ID EST OCULIS INNUERE
(v) to scratch 315	**grater**	SCALPERE
(v) to implore	**regreter**	OPTARE

---

throw out) and an Anglo-French suffix; see MED, s.v., *-ise*. It is related to Anglo-French *geté*, which shares the Latin root of *eiect-*, and which is chiefly attested as an architectural term in John Carpenter's *Liber Albus*, c. 1419 (AND, s.v., *geté*). Hoccleve uses the Middle English term *pentice* to describe the protruding nose of an unattractive lady in a short poem in San Marino, Huntington Library MS HM 744, fol. 52ᵛ (see Langdell, *Thomas Hoccleve's Collected Shorter Poems*, p. 148). There, he celebrates the fact that her *pentice* nose keeps rain out of her mouth (and would do so, even if she were to lie face up towards the sky). **311** *lucrare*: See DMLBS, s.v., *lucrari*, for *lucrare* as a later Latin variant. **312** *gainer*: See AND, s.v., *waynter* and *gaine1*. **313** *guinher*… **314** *innuere*: AND, s.v., *guenyler*, means to wink or blink (cf. DMF, s.v., *guigner*); *oculis innuere* suggests 'to nod with one's eyes'. AND notes that the term occurs in Bibbesworth and 'Nominale sive Verbale'. MS: Between *guinher* and *oculis* is the common abbreviation *i*. (*id est*), used by various glossaries between headword and gloss, though it is only used here and below (*Ja*)in Harley MS 219; cf. CUL Add. 8870 (Baker, 'A French Dictionary'). **316** *regreter*: AND, s.v., *regreter*, means to regret or lament, but it can also mean to invoke or implore in one's lament; in ways that may map onto DMF, s.v., *regretter1*, def. B. DMLBS, s.v., *optare*, seems to mean 'to desire, pray for' more generally.

---

311 gaigner fol. 149ʳ, col. 1

(adj) greater	greign*our* greindre	MAIOR
(adv) today	hui	HODIE
(n) door 320	huys	HOSTI*UM*
(v) to gladden	hetier rehetier	to glade
(adv) immediately, soon	ia ades	now sone
that is (adv) never	Ja	ID *EST* NON
(v) to join 325	ioindre	IUNGERE
(pl n) herbs, grasses	Jontes	wortes
(v) to cackle, to chatter	kaqueter	to kakele

---

317 *greignour*...318 *greindre*: AND, s.v., *graignur*, shows that *greignour* and *greindre* are variants of the same comparative adjective. **323** *ia...sone*: The line contains two French words and their Middle English equivalents. **324** *Ja... non*: AND, s.v., *ja*, def. 6, can function as a temporal adverb to mean 'never'. The gloss *non* could be interpreted as Latin, English, or even French. DMLBS, s.v., *non*, is an all-purpose negative particle. MS: After the headword, the abbreviation *.i.* (*id est*) appears; see *guinher* and *oculis innuere*, a few lines above. **326** *Jontes wortes*: DMF, s.v., *jonc* (a herbaceous water plant or rush); AND, s.v., *junc* (rush or reed); MED, s.v., *wort*, def. 1a ('Any plant or herb; an uncultivated grass, root, or vegetable'). **327** *kaqueter*: See DMF, s.v., *caqueter*; AND lacks a similar entry.

(n) praise	loenge los	}	LAUS
(n) book, or pound 330	liure	a book and a pound	
(pl n) lips	lieures		LABIA
(n) hare	leuure		LEPUS
(n) greyhound	leuerer		LEP*A*RARIUS
(n) hour	leure		HORA
(poss pron) their 335	leure	her*e* thyng	
(n) wolf	lu		LUPUS
he praises	louue		LAUDAT
he rents (or hires)	louue		CONDUCIT

---

331 *lieures*: See the entry below, fol. 150ʳ, col. 2.   **335** *thyng*: MS: This Middle English noun is added in different ink, probably at a later time, to indicate that the possessive pronoun should not be confused with another form of 'here'. It appears hastily executed and may be in Hoccleve's hand; it exhibits a self-dotting *y* and a flat-headed *g* with tail turning counter-clockwise.   **337** *louue laudat*: Third-person singular present active indicative form of AND, s.v., *loer1*, and DMLBS, s.v., *laudare*.   **338** *louue conducit*: Third-person singular present active indicative form of AND, s.v., *loer2*, and DMLBS, s.v., *conducere*.

(n) lark (bird)	aloue	ALAUDA
(adj) rented	340 lowez	hirid
(adj) bound	liez	LIGATUS
(v) to suckle, to give milk to	alaitier	LACTARE
(v) to bind	lier	LIGARE
(v) to remain	Maindre	MANERE
(adj) better	345 miendre	MELIUS
(adj) lesser	meno*u*r	MIN*US*
(n) bawd, procurer/procuress	Makereu^mas makerelle^fe	P*RO*NUBA
(n) hub of a wheel	moel	a cart naue

---

340 *hirid*: MED, s.v., *hiren* (past participle).   **345** *melius*: MS: written over an erasure.   **346** *minus*: MS: written over an erasure.   **347** *Makereumas*…348 *makerellefe*: MS: The abbreviations for masculine (*mas*) and feminine (*fe*) appear interlinearly above each term. AND, s.v., *maquerel*, refers to both masculine and feminine bawds, but compare DMF, s.v., *maquereau* and *maquerelle*.   **348** *pronuba*: DMLBS, s.v., *pronuba*, primarily lists women's roles – bridesmaid, midwife, procuress – but offers one example from 1519 in which the term was used to refer to a man.   **349** *moel*: AND, s.v., *muel1*; see also DMF, s.v., *moel*.

343 lier fol. 149ʳ, col. 2

(n) egg yolk	350	moeille	a yolk*e*
(n) bone marrow		mouelle	MEDULLA
(adj) soft		mole	molle
(adj) wet		moilee	wet
(adj) ground, crushed		molu	grownden
(n) limit, end	355	meute	META
(adj) mute		mue	MUT*US*
(n) mother		miere	M*A*TE*R*
(n) sea		meer	MAR*E*

---

351 *mouelle*: AND, s.v., *meule1*. **352** *mole*: This entry is challenging. I have interpreted the terms as adjectives AND, s.v., *mol1* (cf. DMF, s.v., *mou*), and MED, s.v., *mol*. There is also a Latin adjective *molle*, cited in Du Cange but not DMLBS (which cites only *mollis*, of which *molle* would be a declined form). The headword and gloss might also be seen as nouns to indicate something or someone soft, including an effeminate man, though that meaning is not attested in AND; see MED, s.v., *mol*, def. c; DMLBS, s.v., *mollex* and *mollis,* def. 11; and DMF, s.v., *mou*, def. II.A, which is said to have a neutral value (but see also the gloss for *mol* in Augustine's *Cité de dieu* by Raoul de Presles, linked in the DMF). **354** *molu grownden*: Past participles of AND, s.v., *moudre*, and MED s.v., *grinden*. **355** *meute meta*: AND s.v., *mete1*, and DMLBS, s.v., 1 *meta*, def. 5. The spelling *meute* appears unusual but earns the term its placement in this list.

(n) physician	mire	MEDICUS
(v) to love 360	amer	to loue
(adj) bitter	amer	bittir
(v) to look at, to pay attention to	mirer	SPECULARI
(n) necessity	mestir	NECESSE
(n) artiſtry	mestier	ARTIFICIUM
he changes 365	muet	MUTAT
(num) nine	Noef	NOUEM
(n) ship, boat	Nief	NAUIS
(n) snow	noif	NIX
(adj) natural	Neif	NATIUUS
(pl n) nuts 370	noes	NUCES

---

362 *mirer speculari*: Cf. the previous entry on fol. 148ʳ, col. 3.   **363** *meſtir*: AND, s.v., *meſter1*.   **365** *muet mutat*: Third-person singular active present indicative forms of AND, s.v., *muer1*, and DMLBS, s.v., *mutare*.   **368** *noif*: AND, s.v., *neif1*.   **369** *Neif*: AND, s.v., *naif1*.

(pl n) clouds		nues	NUBES
(pl n) buttons		Noeaus	FIBULE
(adj) drowned		Noiez	SUBMERSUS
(n) marriage		noces	NUPCIE
(adj) naked	375	Nuz	NUDUS
(v) to swim		naire	NATARE
(v) to be born		naistre	NASCI
(n) eye		oeil	OCULUS
[see note]		oil	ITA
(adj) greased, melted	380	oint / sain / fondu	molten

---

373 *Noiez submersus*: Past participles of AND, s.v., *neer1*, and DMLBS, s.v., *submergere*. **379** *ita*: Latin *ita* affirms that 'yes' *oeil* and *oil* are variant spellings. **380** *oint*: Past participle of DMF, s.v., *oindre*, from Latin *unguere* (to grease, to anoint). **381** *sain*: From AND, s.v., *seimer* (to melt, turn to grease).

376 naire fol. 149ʳ, col. 3

(n) goose		ouue	AUCA
(pl n) equals	385	oueles egales	EQUALES
(v) to open		ouurir	AP*ER*IRE
(v) to work		ouerir	OP*E*RARI
(n) pillow		orailler	a pilwer
he hears		ot	AUDIT
(n) man	390	on len ho*m*me	HOMO
(v) to cast a shadow, shade		ombrer	UMBRARE
(v) to shade, to darken		enombrer	OBU*M*BRAR*E*

---

384 *oueles*: Variant of AND, s.v., *uel*, def a.   **387** *ouerir*: AND, s.v., *ovrer1*.
389 *ot audit*: Third-person singular present active indicative of AND, s.v., *oir* and DMLBS, s.v., *audire*.   **390** *on*...392 *homme*: The terms *on*, *en*, and *home* are all variants of AND, s.v., *home*, indicating a man or the indefinite pronoun 'one'.   **394** *enombrer*: According to DMF, s.v., *enombrer*, def 1, and AND, s.v., *enumbrer*, defs 3-4, the term also can describe the process by which Christ was conceived upon the Virgin Mary.

(adj) potent, powerful	395	Peus	POTENS
I stink		pui	FETOR
you stink		pus	TU FETES
he stinks		puit	ILLE FETET
(n) power		peu	POTESTAS
they draw water	400	puissent / espuisent	HAURIUNT
they break, shatter		pecient	FRANGUNT

---

395 *Peus potens*: These are participle forms of AND, s.v., *poer1*, and DMLBS, s.v., *posse*. The French form is a variant of *peu* or *pu*.   **396** *pui fetor*: According to the French in this entry, these should probably both be the first-person singular active indicative forms of 'I stink': *pui* (AND, s.v., *puir*) and *feteo* (DMLBS, s.v., *fetere*), especially since the next two lines offer the correct French and Latin second- and third-person usages. The Latin noun *fetor* (DMLBS, s.v., *foetor* (stench)) must be a copying error, either through eyeskip that led to a mismatched entry and gloss or miscopying the term.   **399** *peu*: The Latin indicates a noun form, but French *peu* tends to be a verb participle form (see above: *peus*). AND, s.v., *pue* is listed as an atypical variant for AND, s.v., *pes1*, which can have the sense of the power or authority to maintain the peace (def. 4); AND, s.v., *poer2*, which has the variant *puer*, denotes power or authority more broadly.   **400** *puissent*...401 *hauriunt*: Third-person plural present active indicative of AND, s.v., *puisier* and *espuiser*, and DMLBS, s.v., *haurire*. The terms can also carry the sense of exhaustion: AND, s.v., puisier (in the past-participle as adjective form); DMF, s.v., *épuiser*; DMLBS, s.v., *haurire*. **402** *pecient frangunt*: Third-person plural present active indicative of AND, s.v., *peçoier*, and DMLBS, s.v., *frangere*.

he will appear	parra	PAREBIT
(n) tar, pitch	pais	PISSA
(n) peace 405	paix	PAX
(n) country, homeland	paijs	PA*T*RIA
(n) weight	pois	PONDUS
(pl n) peas	pois	PISA
(n) thumb	posser	POLLEX
(pres part) weighing 410	poisant	PONDERANS
(adj) heavy	pesant	heuy
(adj) powerful	puissant	POTENS
(pres part) drawing water	puisant	HAURIENS

---

403 *parra parebit*: Third-person singular future active indicative of AND, s.v., *pareir*, and DMLBS, s.v., 1 *parere*.   **404** *pais*: AND, s.v., *pois1*.   **407** *pois*: AND, s.v., *peis1*.   **408** *pois*: AND, s.v., *peis2*.   **409** *pollex*: This gloss could be Latin or English.   **410** *poisant*: AND, s.v., *peisant1*, def. 1.   **411** *pesant*: AND, s.v., *peisant1*, def. 2.

409 posser fol. 149ᵛ, col. 1

(pres part) stinking	puant	FETENS
(pres part) farting 415	peiant	PEDENS
(v) to break, to shatter	pecier	FRANGERE
(v) to draw water	puiser	HAURIRE
(v) to stink	puir	FETERE
(v) to fart	peire	PEDERE
(v) to feed 420	paistre	PASCERE
(v) to knead	pestier	to knede
(v) to cook, to bake	Quir pestier	PISTRIRE
(pl n) branches	Ramsiaux	RAMUNCULI

---

420 *paistre pascere*: AND, s.v., *paistre*, and DMLBS, s.v., *pascere* can mean to feed humans or animals, and both can indicate physical or spiritual nourishment. **421** *pestier*: AND, s.v., *pesteri*, notes that the Latin source verb *pistare* has a primary sense of 'to pound or grind', with secondary senses of 'to bake' and 'to knead' (DMLBS, s.v., *pistare*). See also *pestier* in the next entry and on fol. 150ʳ, col. 1. **422** *Quir pestier*: By grouping AND, s.v., *pesteri*, with AND, s.v., *cuirei* (to cook or bake), the glossary provides context for reading *pestier* as 'to bake'. See also *pestier* above and on fol. 150ʳ, col. 1. **423** *Ramsiaux ramunculi*: AND, s.v., *raimsel*; DMLBS, s.v., *ramunculus*.

(pl n) brambles	**Rounces**	VEPRES
(pl n) streams 425	**Ruissiaux**	RIUOLI
(v) to blush, to redden	**Rouger**	to wexe reed
(v) to mark with a line or stripe	**Raier**	to score
(n) a line or stripe	**Raye**	a score
(v) to scrape, to erase	**Rere**	RADERE
(v) to turn green 430	**Rauerder**	VIRESCERE
(v) to seize, to rape	**Rauoier**	RAPERE
(n) scab	**Roigne**	SCABIES
(v) to lock, to fasten	**Sarrer**	SERARE
(v) to drag, to pull	**sachier** 435 **traire** }	TRAHERE

---

425 *Ruissiaux*: AND, s.v., *russel1*; DMLBS, s.v., *rivolus*. **426** *Rouger*: AND, s.v., *roujoier*; DMF, s.v., *rougir*. **429** *Rere*: AND, s.v., *rere1*. **432** *scabies*: The gloss might be read as Latin or English; see also fol. 148ᵛ, col. 1. **434** *sachier*: AND, s.v., *saker*.

[see note]	soiourer	SEPARARE
(v) to scour, to polish	Escurer	to shour*e*
[see note]	signer	CINGERE
(n) stool	scelle	SCABELLU*M*
(adj) white-haired, gray 440	Chanuz	hoor
(n) mouse	soriz	MUS
(n) to saw, to chop wood	cier	SCINDER*E*
(n) a saw	Sye	a sawe
(conj) if	Se	SI

---

436 *soiourer separare*: There has apparently been a copying error or omitted entry. AND, s.v., *sujurer*, and DMF, s.v., *séjourner*, mean to stay behind or tarry; the terms have a cognate in DMLBS, s.v., *sojornare*; or DMLBS, s.v., *sperare* (to wait for something) may have been intended. DMLBS, s.v., *separare*, means to divide or separate (cf. AND, s.v., *severer*). **437** *to shoure*: MED, s.v., *scouren*, v. 2. **438** *signer cingere*: A copying error has mis-matched terms. AND, s.v., *signer* means to mark or designate, which was probably meant to be paired with DMLBS, s.v., *signare*. DMLBS, s.v., *cingere*, which means to gird or to encircle, probably should have been paired with a form of AND, s.v., *ceindre1*. **441** *mus*: This gloss is likely Latin, though *mus* is a variant of MED, s.v., *mous*. **442** *cier*: AND, s.v., *sier1*. **444** *Se si*: AND, s.v., *si2*; DMLBS, s.v., *si*.

440 Chanuz fol. 149ᵛ, col. 2

(adv) so, thus	445	Si	SIC
[see note]		serrez	SEDIBIT*UR*
(n) fat, grease		sain	grece
(n) suet, tallow		sieu	talwh*e*
(n) soap		savon	sope
(n) a mower, reaper	450	siour	a scherer*e*
(pl n) scissors, shears		siselles	sheres
(v) to sweat, perspire		suer	SUDAR*E*
(v) to follow		suir	SEQUI
(v) to soil, to befoul		Toiller	—
(v) to fit, to fashion (into)	455	tailler	APTARE

---

445 *Si sic*: AND, s.v., *si1*; DMLBS, s.v., *sic*.   **446** *serrez sedibitur*: A copying error has mis-matched terms. The pairing of AND, s.v., *serrer1* (to lock) and *serrer2* (to saw) suggests that we might be missing forms of DMLBS, s.v., *serrare* (to saw) or *serare* (to lock). The term *sedebitur* derives from DMLBS, s.v., *sedere*, which can mean, among other things, 'to sit', so perhaps a form of AND, s.v., *seer1* (to sit) was its intended entry term.   **450** *siour...scherere*: AND, s.v., *sior*; MED, s.v., *sherer(e*. See fol. 151ʳ, col. 3.

(v) to remove, to take away	toller } ouster	DEPONERE
(v) to strike	torcher	PERCUTERE
(v) to twist, to wring	tortir	to wrynge
(v) to deceive 460	trainer	DECIPERE
(v) to cross, to thwart	trauerser	ouerthwerte
(prep) across	a trauers	EXTRANSUERSO
(adv) appropriately, suitably	attaignaument	ATTINGENTER

456 *toller*... **457** *deponere*: See above, fol. 148ʳ, col. 3, which features a cluster of *ouster*, *tollir*, and *bouter*, glossed by *deponere*. **458** *torcher*: AND, s.v., *torcher* can also mean 'to wipe'; see below in the list of 'verba equivoca' on fol. 150ʳ, col. 1. **459** *tortir*: AND, s.v., *tortreɪ*; see fol. 150ʳ, col. 1. **460** *trainer*: Something has gone awry in copying. This might be a misreading or variant of AND, s.v., *trahirɪ* (to betray, to deceive), or a verb constructed from AND, s.v., *traine2* (deceit, treachery). An eyeskip error is also possible: AND, s.v., *trainer* means to pull or drag and could have been paired with a relevant gloss, then followed by a separate entry for *trahir* and *decipere*. **461** *trauerser ouerthwerte*: See MED, s.v., *overthwerten*. This is a rare instance in which Hoccleve deploys a gloss that represents a Middle English infinitive without including 'to'. **462** *extransuerso*: DMLBS, s.v., *transversus*, def. 3. **463** *attaignaument attingenter*: AND, s.v., *atteignaument*, is the adverb from AND, s.v., *atteindre*, and the Latin root, DMLBS, s.v., *attingere*, which generally means 'to touch' (literally or figuratively) or 'to reach'; the figurative sense leads to the notion of being appropriate or suitable. There is no adverbial form *attingenter* listed in the DMLBS, but the construction is analogous to its synonym in DMLBS, s.v., *convenienter*, and the term is found in medieval Latin from the Netherlands, according to *Lexicon latinitatis nederlandicae medii aevi*, ed. J. W. Fuchs and

(v) to dye, to color	taindre	TINGERE
(v) to stretch 465	tendre	TENDERE
(v) to shear, to clip	tondre	TONDERE
(v) to reach, to touch	atteindre	ATTINGERE
(v) to await, to expect	attendre	EXPECTARE
(v) to turn, to reverse	verser	VERTERE
(v) to break wind, to fart 470	vesser	to fyste
(v) to go	vais	VADO
(n) fly	vole	MUSCA

---

others, 11 vols (Brill, 1977–2005), A.679. I am grateful to the press reviewer for this reference. **464** *taindre*: AND, s.v., *teindre2*. **465** *tendre tendere*: See AND, s.v., *tendre1*, and DMLBS, s.v., *tendere*, for a wider range of overlapping meanings, including to extend, to reach, to proceed, to offer (for sale). **467** *atteindre attingere*: See AND, s.v., *atteindre*, and DMLBS, s.v., *attingere*, for a wider range of meanings. **468** *attendre*: AND, s.v., *atendre1*. **470** *vesser*: DMF, s.v., *vessir* (no attestation in AND). See also *vesser* on fol. 148ʳ, col. 3. **471** *vais vado*: First-person singular present indicative of AND, s.v., *aler1*, and DMLBS, s.v., *vadere*. **472** *vole musca*: DMLBS, s.v., *musca*, confirms that this must refer to a flying insect. AND lacks an entry for *vole*, but AND, s.v., *vol1*, offers noun usages as 'flight' and 'wings' (cf. DMF, s.v., *vol*), and AND, s.v.,

472 vole fol. 149ᵛ, col. 3

(adj) hairy		veluz	HIRSUT*US*
(n) spring (season)		ver	VERNUS
(n) gray fur	475	vair	gray
Here follow ambiguous words		**HIC SECUNT*UR* VERBA EQUIUOCA**	
(v) to fill completely and to water horses		Abuurer	P*ER*IMPLERE ET ADAQU*A*RE EQUOS
(prep) beneath and along		Aual	deius *et* p*a*rmy
(v) to learn and to teach	480	Aprendre	ADISCE*R*E *ET* DOCE*R*E
(conj) on the contrary and (conj/adv) before		ancois	YM*M*O *ET* AN*TEQU*A*M*

---

palevole, acknowledges that the term *vole* there may mean to fly; cf. *paleuole* on fol. 151ʳ, col. 3.   **475**   *vair gray*: AND, s.v., *vair1*, and MED, s.v., *grei*, n.2.   **476**   *Hic…equiuoca*: MS: The initial *H* has decorative flourishes and is the height of about three regular glossary lines; the heading is written in a more formal script. In this section, multiple glosses are given immediately after the headword; when they carry over on the next line, there is a bracket at right to indicate visually that those lines are one entry and its glosses.   **477** *Abuurer*: AND, s.v., *enbeverer*, records the meaning 'to fill with liquid' (def. 2) and a substantive infinitive pertaining to watering livestock; see also DMF, s.v., *abreuver* and *abreuveur*.   **479** *Aual*: AND, s.v., *aval* (adv), means underneath or down below; *aval* (prep), can mean 'down (along)' or 'around, about'. | *deius… parmy*: This gloss is French; see AND, s.v., *dejus* and *parmi*.

(adv) immediately and continuously	ades 485	tost *et* continuelm*en*t
(v) to love and (adj) bitter	amer	DILIGER*E* *ET* AMARU*M*
(n) pin and ankle	Cheuill*e*	a pin *and* an ancle
(v) to compare and to be punished for	comp*a*rer	SIM*U*LARE *ET* LUER*E*
(n) horn and tippett (headdress)	490 cornet	an horn *and* a tipet
(v) to suffer and to think	compasser	soeffrer *et* penser
(v) to play and to take pleasure	esbatre	LUDERE *ET* GAUDER*E*

---

484 *tost*...485 *continuelment*: Both glosses are in French: AND, s.v., *tost2* and *continuelment*; *tost* may also be associated with a variant of Latin *tot*. **486** *amer*: See also the two entries for *amer* on fol. 149ʳ, col. 2. **488** *Cheuille*: See also 'ma cheuille' on fol. 150ʳ, col. 3. **491** *soeffrer*...*penser*: The glosses are French verbs: AND, s.v., *suffrir* and *penser*. See also *Compasser* on fol. 147ᵛ, col. 3. **492** *esbatre*...*gaudere*: AND, s.v., *esbatreı*, means 'to divert' but also 'to have sexual intercourse'. Both meanings are attested in Jean Gessler, ed. *Manière de langage* (L'Edition Universelle, 1934), p. 65, in the 1396 text (hereafter Gessler, *Manière*). See also Kristol, *Manières*, 15.7 and 22.33. DMLBS, s.v., *gaudere*, does not record an explicitly sexual usage, though one might be inferred from 'to take pleasure or delight', and the noun form *gaudium* (orgasm), as treated in J. N. Adams, *Latin Sexual Vocabulary* (The Johns Hopkins University Press, 1982), pp. 197–98.

[see note]		sesbatre	IDE*M*
(v) to release and to forgive		finer	SOLU*ERE* ET DIMITT*ERE*
(v) to forsake and to go insane	495	forsener	forsake and go wood
it is necessary and it is lacking		faut	OPORTET *ET* DEFICIT
(adj) noxious and arrogant		fumous	FUMOS*US* ET SUPERB*US*

---

493 *sesbatre*: *Idem* indicates 'the same' (meanings as *esbatre*). The reflexive verb seems to suggest 'to amuse oneself' or 'have sex', not necessarily 'to masturbate'. The usage in Gessler, *Manière*, p. 65, clearly indicates a partner: 'le signeur s'esbat et esjoit atant avecque s'amie'.   **494** *finer…dimittere*: AND, s.v., *finer1* and *finer3*, suggest the meaning 'to pay' in the sense of concluding a bargain or resolving a debt. In canon law, 'solvo et dimitto' or 'solvit et dimittit' is a legal formula for 'release and forgive', frequently used in indulgences. See also DMLBS, s.v., *solvere* and *dimittere*.   **496**   *faut*: AND, s.v., *faillir*. **497** *fumosus…superbus*: AND, s.v., *fumous*, offers only 'fumous, generating (injurious) exhalations in the human body', with a sole citation from the Waterford French translation of the *Secretum Secretorum*. The terms 'fumositees' (fumes, vapors) and 'fumoses' appear in the *Secretum Secretorum* on fol. 98ᵛ of Harley 219. DMF, s.v., *fumeux*, acknowledges a figurative sense that could define a person as choleric or quick to anger. DMLBS, s.v., *fumosus*, encompasses both meanings related to injurious fumes and anger. The gloss *superbus* calls attention to the figurative meaning. See also FEW, s.v., *fumeux*, which suggests that the vapours might cause intoxication, leading to an adjective that means intoxicated.

(v) to drain away	fluir	to welke *and* to fade
it withers and fades	fleint	welkith *and* fadith
(adv) much and [for a] long time	500 Guerres	MULTUM *ET* LONGUM T*EM*P*U*S
(v) to provide and....	garnir	MUNIRE *ET* —
(adv) never and now	Ja | non	NU*N*QUAM *ET* IAM
(adv) slowly and with difficulty	Enuis	TARDE *ET* VIX
(adj) tame and secret	priuee	tame *and* secree

---

498 *fluir*: AND, s.v., *fluer*, and DMF, s.v., *fluir*, def. B, suggest to drain or to drain away. | *to*¹...*fade*: MED, s.v., *welken*, v.1, can mean to wither, dry up, shrivel, or waste away; and *faden*, v. 1, indicates a loss of brilliance, color, freshness, strength or vitality. **499** *fleint*: The third-person active indicative conjugation of *flenir*, which may be a variant or corruption of AND, s.v., *feindre*; see discussion of *flenir* on fol. 148ᵛ, col. 3. **500** *Guerres*: AND, s.v., *gueres*, defs 1 and 2. **501** *garnir munire*: AND, s.v., *garnir1*, and DMLBS, s.v., *munire*, both mean to provide or supply. AND, s.v., *garnir1*, can also mean: to warn; to advise; or, reflexively, to pay attention, to prepare oneself. AND, s.v., *garnir2*, is a cross-reference to the noun form, s.v., *gerner1*, which refers to a granary or storehouse. **502** *Ja...iam*: MS: There are about three lines of empty space below this last entry; on the next line is the catchword: *enuis*. **503** *Enuis*: AND, s.v., *enviz*. **504** *priuee*: AND, s.v., *privé1*, typically refers to private items or persons, but when used of animals, it indicates 'tame, domesticated'.

---

503 Enuis fol. 150ʳ, col. 1

(v) to bake and to knead	505	pestier	to bake *and* knede
(n) ray of the sun / a tally mark and a stripe		Raye	RADIUS SOLIS / a score and a stryke
(v) to say and to sound		soner	LOQUI ET PULSARE
(v) to bake and to cook		quir	PISTRIRE ET COQUERE
(v) to lock away and to lock		sarrer	to make fast and to loke
(adj, n) healthy and male saints	510	sanis	SANUS ET SANCTI
(pl n) female saints and bells		saintes	SANCTE ET CAMPANE

---

505 *pestier*: See *pestier*, above, fol. 149ᵛ, col. 1. **506** *Raye...stryke*: See AND, s.v., *rai1* (beam of light) and *rai2* (a stripe). The Latin translates the first sense, and the second gloss is English. MED, s.v., *strike*, can refer to streaks in fabric, hence my gloss of 'stripe', but MED, s.v., *score*, seems less directly related, except that it can refer to a tally stick, and presumably in this case, the marks made on one. See also fol. 149ᵛ, col. 1. **508** *quir*: See *Quir pestier*, above, fol. 149ᵛ, col. 1. **509** *sarrer*: AND, s.v., *serrer1*, means both to secure a door by locking it and to lock someone or something away; see MED, s.v., *fast(e*, adv, def. 2, 3, for its use for securing, enclosing or imprisoning. See also *serrez*, fol. 149ᵛ, col. 2. **510** *sancti*: The Latin *sancti* is in the nominative plural masculine form, so 'holy men' or male saints; the expected adjective form for 'holy' that would match *sanus* (healthy) would be *sanctus*. **511** *saintes*: AND, s.v., *seint1*, and *seint1*. The Latin *sanctae* and *campanae* are nominative plural feminine forms.

you will know, you will smell, and you will touch	Tu sentiras	SCIES ODORABIS *ET* PALPABIS
(v) to tremble and deceive	tremeler	TREM*ERE ET* DECIPERE
(n) time and weather	temps	TEMP*US ET* TEMP*ER*IES
(n) edge and (adj) sharp and (n or adj) cutting 515	trenchant	egge and sharp and kuttyng*e*
(v) to strike and to wipe clean	torcher	P*E*RCUTERE *ET* T*ER*G*ERE*
(v) to twist/squeeze and twist/bend	tortir	to wrynge *and* wrythe

---

512 *sentiras*: AND, s.v., *sentir1* (cf. DMF, s.v., *sentir*); DMLBS, s.v., *scire*. **513** *tremeler*: See AND, s.v., *trembler2* (to tremble), and DMF, s.v., *tremeler*, def. B. (to deceive). **515** *trenchant…kuttynge*: AND, s.v., *trencher*, lists definitions for the verb, adjective and noun forms. The adjective sense of 'sharp' can also include a figurative sense of 'keen' or 'perceptive' or 'painful'. It is unclear whether the English gloss, MED, s.v., *cuttinge*, refers to the action of cutting, to an incision or something cut off, or to an adjectival use. See fol. 147ᵛ, col. 1, *trenchant*, for a Latin gloss. **516** *torcher*: See also above, fol. 149ᵛ, col. 2. **517** *tortir*: DMF, s.v., *tortir*, means to twist, wring or bend. MED, s.v., *wringen* and *writhen* have similar meanings of 'to twist', but 'wringen' usually has a notion of squeezing, and 'writhen' can also mean 'to twist' in the sense of to intertwine or bend. See also above, fol. 149ᵛ, col. 2.

(v) to vow and to recognize	vouer	VOU*ERE ET* RECOGNOSCERE
(prep) in	ou	IN
(adv, rel pr, conj) where 520	ou	VBI
(conj) or	ou	VEL
What do you do?	Qe faites vo*us*	what do ye
How are you doing?	coment faites vous	how faren ye
It is very cold	Il fait grant froit	it is gret cold

---

518 *vouer*: AND, s.v., *vouer2*, means to vow or promise (cf. DMF, s.v., *vouer1*); AND, s.v., *avouer2*, def. 2, includes not only 'to vow' but also 'to recognize, admit (responsibility for), acknowledge', which overlaps with DMLBS, s.v., *recognoscere*, defs 2-5. AND, s.v., *vouer1*, and DMF, s.v., *vouer2* are defined as 'to invoke' and 'to call to court', respectively, which may evoke legal meanings associated with DMLBS, s.v., *recognoscere* (defs 1, 5). **519** *ou in*: In this enclitic form, the preposition *en* followed by the article *le* become *ou*. | *ou...*521 *vel*: MS: These three short words and glosses occupy one line in the manuscript with faint dividing lines between them. The term *vbi* is written over an erasure that has partially erased the divider after it. To accommodate the modern edition formatting, I have grouped them closely together instead. | *in*: I have assumed that this gloss is Latin, to match 'ubi' and 'vel', though it could just as easily be recognized as English. **522** *faites*: This and the two subsequent entries offer various uses of AND, s.v., *faire*, including the impersonal form.

Names of the parts of the human body 525	**NO*MI*NA MEMBROR*UM* HUMANI CORPORIS**	
my head	Ma teste	MEU*M* CAPUT
my hair	mes chiueux	MEI C*RI*NES
my forehead	ma front	MEA FRONS
my ears 530	mes oreilles	MEE AURES
my eyes	mes yeux	MEI OCULI
my eyelids	mes surcilz	MEE PALPEBRE
my eyebrows	mes surcilles	MEA SUPERCILIA
my nose	mon nies	MEUS NAS*US*

525 *Nomina...* **526** *corporis*: The headwords and glosses in this section have substantial overlap with CUL Add. 8870, fol. 30ʳ; see Baker, 'A French Vocabulary', pp. 85–86. See also Kristol, *Manières*, pp. 3–4 and 51–52, for similar lists of Anglo-French terms. MS: When glosses carry over onto the next line, there is a bracket at the right. This heading, which takes up two lines, split after *membrorum*, has a bracket with a decorative flourish at the top and is written in a more formal script. **532** *mes...palpebre*: In Baker, 'A French Vocabulary', p. 85, Latin *palpebre* (eyelids) glosses the French cognate *mes paupiers*, followed by 'mes cilles mea cilia' (eyelashes) and 'mes furcilles (sic) mea supersilia' (eyebrows). AND, s.v., *surcil*, attests meanings of either eyebrow or eyelid; cf. AND, s.v., *surciller*.

525 Nomina fol. 150ʳ, col. 2

my nostrils 535	mes narins	MEI NARES
my nasal cartilage	ma tendrou*n*	my gristel
my cheeks	mes iouues	MEE FAUCES
my mouth	ma bouche	MEU*M* OS
my lips	mes lieures	MEA LABIA
my teeth 540	mes dens	MEE DENTES
my tongue	ma langue	MEA LINGUA
my chin	ma menton	MEU*M* MENTUM
my throat	ma gorge	MEU*M* GUTT*U*R
my neck	mon col	MEU*M* COLLUM
my shoulders 545	mes espaules	MEE SPATULE
the tendon at the back of the neck	le vendon	the faxwax

---

536 *ma...gristel*: Compare Baker, 'A French Vocabulary', p. 85.   **537** *iouues*: AND, s.v., *joe1*.   **539** *lieures*: See the similar entry on fol. 149ʳ, col. 1.   **546** *faxwax*: MED, s.v., *fax-wax*.

my shoulder blade	mon blazon	—
my armpits	mes asselles	MEE ASSELLE
my arms	mes bras	MEA BRACHIA
my upper arms 550	mes mahutes	—
my elbows	mes coutes	MEI CUBITI
my hands	mes mains	MEE MANUS
my fingers	mes dois	MEI DIGITI
my palm	ma paume	MEA PALMA
my nails 555	mes vngles	MEI VNGUES
my joints	mes iointes	MEE IUNCTAE
my cheſt	ma poitrine	MEUM PECTUS

---

547 *blazon*: AND, s.v., *blason*. Cf. Baker, 'A French Vocabulary', p. 85: 'mon blason my schulder bone'. **548** *asselles...asselle*: AND, s.v., *esseler*; DMLBS, s.v., *axilla*. **550** *mahutes*: AND, s.v., *mahuſtre*; DMF, s.v., *maheutre*; in Baker, 'A French Vocabulary', p. 85, 'mes mahutres' is also unglossed. **555** *mei*: MS: *i* written over *e*.

552 mes mains fol. 150ʳ, col. 3

my breasts	mes mamelles	MEE MAMILLE
my breasts (women's)	mes tetes 560	IDEM SUNT MULIERUM
my sides	mes coustees	my sydes
my flanks	mes flanks	my laskes
my back	mon dors	MEUM DORSUM
my bones	mes os	MEA OSSA
my belly, womb 565	mon ventre	MEUS VENTER
my navel	mon vmbril	MEUS VMBELICUS
the spine	leschyn	the rigbon
my penis	mon vit	MEUM VERETRUM

---

559 *tetes*: AND, s.v., *teteɪ* (breast, nipple) attests only Baker, 'A French Vocabulary', p. 86. DMF, s.v., *tette*, indicates the term was primarily used for the breasts of animals. | *idem ... 560 mulierum*: 'The same belonging to women', an idiomatic Latin use of the genitive. The gloss in Baker, 'A French Vocabulary', p. 86, is 'mamille mulierum'. **562** *flanks*: AND, s.v., *flanc*. | *laskes*: MED, s.v., *leske*. **567** *leschyn*: Elision of *l'eschine*; see AND, s.v., *eschine*.

my pubes	mon penyl	MEUS PECTEN
my testicles 570	mes coillons	MEI TESTIC*U*LI
my anus	mon cuel	MEUS CULUS
my buttocks	mes hanches	my buttokes
my thighs	me quysses	my thyghes
my groin	ma lene	—
my knees 575	mes genoilles	MEA GENUA
my legs	mes iambes	MEE TIBIE
the hamstring	le garet de ma iambe	the hamme
the calf	le assure	the calf

---

569 *penyl*: AND, s.v., *penil1*: 'pubes, lower part of the abdomen above the genitals'. DMLBS, s.v., *pecten*, def. 2, attests 'public region', but see LSLD, s.v., *pecten*, for 'The hair of the pubes'. Baker, 'A French Vocabulary', p. 86, offers the modern gloss 'loins'. Critten, *French Lessons*, pp. 56–57, translates the French term as *pubes*.   **574** *ma lene*: This entry attaches the possessive pronoun *ma* to the noun *aine* with lexicalized pronoun (*l'aine* becomes *lene*). See AND, s.v., *aine2* (groin), which recognizes *lene* as an Anglo-Norman form, so this should not be taken as an error; the only citation appears in the *Manière*, ed. Gessler, p. 46. In Baker, 'A French Vocabulary', p. 86, *ma lene* is glossed as *thihole* (MED, s.v., *thigh*, def. 1a, groin area).   **577** *le…iambe*: Literally: 'the ham of my leg'.

my feet	mes pies	MEI PEDES
my ankle 580	ma cheuill*e*	MEA CAUILLA
my heel	mon talou*n*	MEUS TALUS
my toes	mes artols	MEI ARTIC*U*LI
the sole of my foot	la plane de mon pie	PLANTA MEI PEDIS
The interior of the body 585	**INTERIORA CORPORIS**	
the brain	le ceruel	CEREBRUM
the larynx, Adam's apple	le gorget / le gorgat	thretboll*e*

---

580 *cheuille*: See also the entries on fol. 148ᵛ, col. 2, and fol. 149ᵛ, col. 3. **583** *la*…584 *pedis*: MS: This last entry has the French on the final line of the column, with the Latin on an additional line below, linked by an *L*-shaped bracket. **585** *Interiora corporis*: In this section, some apparently Latin glosses contain terms that pass relatively unchanged into English and/or French, e.g., *cerebrum, splen, vene*. The notes point out such ambiguous glosses. There is also substantial overlap with CUL Add. 8870, fols 30ʳ⁻ᵛ; see Baker, 'A French Vocabulary', pp. 86–87. MS: The initial *I* has a decorative approach stroke and tail, and the heading is written in a more formal script. Two blank lines follow the heading. **586** *cerebrum*: This medical term can be Latin or English. **587** *le*…588 *thretebolle*: AND, s.v., *gorgite*; DMF, s.v., *gargate*. MED, s.v., *throte-bolle*.

585 Interiora corporis fol. 150ᵛ, col 1

the heart		le cuer	COR
the liver	590	le foye	EPAR
the lung		le pulmoun	PULMO
the spleen or diaphragm		le marrite	midryfe
the spleen		le splen	SPLEN
the stomach		le stomac	STOMACUS
the gall-bladder	595	le fiel	FEL
he kidneys		les reynes	RENES
the bowels		les boiaux	VISCERA

---

590 *epar*: This medical term can be Latin or English; see MED, s.v., *epar*. See also fol. 148ᵛ, col. 3.   **592** *le…midryfe*: First, Hoccleve (or his source) has elided the possessive pronoun *ma* and headword *rate* into *marrite* and added the article *le*. Compare Baker, 'A French Vocabulary', p. 87: *la rate* with gloss *mydryf*. Second, modern dictionaries indicate uncertainty about these terms. AND, s.v., *rate1*, traditionally means spleen, and MED, s.v., *mid-rif*, traditionally means diaphragm, but Middle English glosses to Anglo-Norman language-learning texts suggest the conflation of these terms (e.g., Bibbesworth and 'Nominale sive Verbale'). In CUL Add. 8870, fol. 30ᵛ, the term appears with the nerves a few lines below; Hoccleve (or his source) instead places it between the lung and spleen.   **593** *splen²*: The gloss could be Latin or English.   **595** *le…fel*: Both terms can also mean gall or bile.   **596** *renes*: This gloss could be Latin or English.

the bladder	la vessie	VESICA
the skin	la pel	PELLIS
(pl n) veins 600	veynes	VENE
the nerves/tendons	les nerfs	NERUI
the arteries	les arteries	ART*ERI*E
The four humours choler, blood, phlegm, melancholy 605	les quatre humo*ur*s Chalo*ur* / sanc / fleume / malencolie	—
(n) small purse	tassete	a pouche
a hood	vn chape*rou*n	CAPICIU*M*

---

598 *vesica*: This gloss is Latin, but compare MED, s.v., *vesic(e*. **600** *vene*: This gloss might be Latin or English. **601** *les…nerui*: AND, s.v., *nerf*, warns that *nerf*, like its counterparts in Latin and English, could mean nerve or tendon, so especially absent context, it can be difficult to tell which is intended. This gloss is likely Latin, but MED, s.v., *nerve* attests 'nervi' and 'nerf' as variant spellings. **602** *arterie*: This gloss is Latin (since the headword is also a nominative plural), but compare MED, s.v., *arterie*. **603** *les…605 malencolie*: MS: The bracket in the manuscript links the two lines that name the humours. **606** *pouche*: MS: Two blank lines with erasures follow this entry. After a similar list of medical terms in CUL Add. 8870, fol. 30ᵛ, a heading classifies the words that follow: 'vestimenta' (clothing). There is substantial overlap between CUL Add. 8870 and Harley 219 in the list of clothing items, with a lesser degree of shared terms in subsequent categories, which CUL Add. 8870 identifies with headings that Harley 219 omits. See Baker, 'A French Vocabulary', pp. 87–95.

a liripipe	vn cornet	LIRIPIPIUM
a hat	vn chapel	CAPELLA
a cap 610	vn barette	TENA
a felt cap	vn pilio*n*	PILIUS
a cap, hood	vne coife	—
a shirt	vne chemise	—
the breeches	les brais	BRACCE
a doublet, jerkin 615	vn corsette	—
a coat, tunic	vne cote	—
an outer (great) coat	vne hopelande	TOGA
an outer coat	vn tabard	—
a close-fitting tunic or doublet	vn Jupou*n*	—

---

614 *les… bracce*: See also the entry on fol. 148ᵛ, col. 1. **619** *Jupoun*: AND, s.v., *jupon*.

611 vn pilioun fol. 150ᵛ, col. 2

a quilted doublet, paltock 620	vn purpoint	—
a doublet	vn doublet	—
a mantle	vn mantel	—
a pair of mittens	vne paire de mitaynes	—
(pl n) gloves	Gans	CIROTECE
(pl n) hose 625	chauces	CALIGE
(pl n) shoes	soliers	SOTULARES
(pl n) boots	Botes	OCREE
(pl n) spurs	esporons	CALCARIA
a hairnet, headdress	vn reiteal	a calle

---

623 *mitaynes*: MS: The final letter extends into the third column. **629** *reiteal*: The term likely derives from DMF, s.v., *reteɪ* or AND, s.v., *reiɪ* (net) and a diminutive ending, much like DMLBS, s.v., *reticulum* (def. 1b: hairnet) is constructed from *rete* and the diminutive suffix *–culum*. See also as a plausible source, DMF, s.v., *retenal*, which refers to any device that binds or holds something else. | *a calle*: MED, s.v., *calle*, def. a (hairnet or headdress).

a hairnet	630	vn cordelet pur chiueux	—
(pl n) head coverings, kerchiefs		Couerchiefs	—
(pl n) hairpins		espingles	—
a tapestry		vn doseour	—
a bench-cover		vn bankeour	—
a cushion	635	vn quarreau	a quisshyn
a bench		vn banc	—
a table		vne table	—

---

630 *vn...chiueux*: A similar entry 'un cordellot pur chiveux', appears in Baker, 'A French Vocabulary', p. 88, where the glosses are DMLBS, s.v., *reticulum* (hairnet), and *couvrechyefs*. Baker's is the only attestation for AND, s.v., *cordellot*. MS: *chiueux* runs over onto the next line, with a connecting bracket. **632** *espingles*: DMF, s.v., *épingle*, denotes hairpins or a pin for clothing; context here suggests hairdressing; cf. AND, s.v., *espinel1*. See also *espingles* on fol. 148ᵛ, col. 2. MS: There are four blank lines following this entry. After a similar list of medical terms in CUL Add. 8870, fol. 30ᵛ, there is a heading 'Aula' (Hall) and list of furniture and domestic items, some of which are also represented in Harley 219. **633** *doseour*: DMF, s.v., *doseur* (tapestry, cushion for the back of an armchair or bench), and *dossierer* (tapestry that could be used on a wall, an altar, or furniture); Baker, 'A French Vocabulary', p. 88, provides the modern gloss 'dossal (wall-tapestry)'. Cf. MED, s.v., *doser*. **635** *quisshyn*: MS: The final two letters extend into the third column.

637 vne table fol. 150ᵛ, col. 3

a three-legged stool or seat	vn brichet	a trestle
a stool, etc.	vn scelle	a stool ET ALIA
a (maple) wood drinking bowl 640	vn madre	a maser
a silver cup	vn tasse dargent	a pece
a goblet	vn gobre	PECIA ROTUNDA
a cup, bowl, goblet	vne cupe	CUPA
a drinking cup	vn verre	VITRUM
a pan 645	vne paelle	PATELLA
a frying pan	vn lechefryt	a fryyngpanne

---

639 *a…alia*: MS: The Latin is an *et* abbreviation then *al* with a suspension mark; there is a *nota* mark or otiose stroke at the end of the line. I take the abbreviation to indicate *et alia* (and other [seats]), because I have not located another logical translation of AND, s.v., *scelle*, that begins with *al-* and suits the context of these domestic items. CUL Add. 8870, fol. 30ᵛ, glosses *scelle* with Latin *scabellum*; see also *scelle*, above, fol. 149ᵛ, col. 1.   **640** *madre*: DMF, s.v., *madre* and AND, s.v., *mazer*, def. 2, refer both to maple wood and the drinking vessel made from it.   **641** *pece*: MED, s.v., *pece*, def. 4b (drinking vessel, wine cup). The Latin *pecia*, in the next gloss, is the root for the English term. **642** *gobre*: Copying confusion of *l* for *r* in AND, s.v., *goblet*.   **643** *vne…cupa*: DMLBS, s.v., *cupa*, indicates a vat or tub. AND, s.v., *cuppe*, has those meanings but can also indicate a cup, bowl, or goblet; the surrounding entries have guided my modern gloss.   **646** *fryyngpanne*: MS: The English term is split over two lines, with a linking bracket.

a three-legged tripod, trivet	vn troipie	TRIPES
a grill	vne graille	CRATICULA
a bellows	vn sufflet	a belwe
a fleshhook 650	vn crooke	a fleshhooke
(pl n) tongs	Molais ⎱ tenelles ⎰	tonges
a tub	vn cake	a tubbe
a vat	vne keuue	a fat
a bucket 655	vn siel	SITULA
(n) baker	Bolengier	PISTOR
a ſtrainer	vn estamyn	a streynour

---

647 *tripes*: DMLBS, s.v., *tripes*. **651** *Molais*…**652** *tenelles*: AND, s.v., *tenail2*; DMF, s.v., *molet2*. CUL Add. 8870, fol. 31ʳ (Baker, 'A French Vocabulary', p. 90), contains an entry for *un peyr dez tenelles* but not *molais* or a variant of *molet*. **655** *siel*: MS: The second letter is blurred or damaged but appears to have the approach stroke of an *i*, and *siel* would be a variant for AND, s.v., *seil1* (bucket) and the gloss DMLBS, s.v., *situla* (bucket). **656** *Bolengier pistor*: See also the entry on fol. 147ᵛ, col. 2. **657** *eſtamyn*: DMF, s.v., *étamine*, def. c, can mean a specific cloth used for filtering, or a woollen cloth or garment; AND, s.v., *eſtamine*, only attests the meaning of woollen garment.

(n) cook		Quisiner	COCUS
(n) bridle		vne brinde ⎫	FRENUM
	660	vn frein ⎭	
(n) halter		vn cheuestre	CAPISTRUM
(n) crupper		vn culer	a croper
(pl n) ſtirrups		estruz	stiropes
(n) heifer		Joeuece	a hefre
a sow	665	vne truye	a sowe

---

659 *vne*…660 *frenum*: CUL Add. 8870, fol. 31ʳ, also defines *brinde* only with *frenum*, adding *vn freint pur vn mulet* (a bridle for a mule) on the next line. Baker, 'A French Vocabulary', p. 90, notes that 'bit' is a better gloss for 'brinde' and posits a missing word, but perhaps the source manuscript, like Harley 219, collapsed the complexities of the equipment. **663** *eſtruz*: AND, s.v., *eſtriu*. **664** *Joeuece*: AND, s.v., *juvence*. Cf. CUL Add. 8870, fol. 31ʳ (Baker, 'A French Vocabulary', p. 91): 'vne iuvece'.

665 vne truye fol. 151ʳ, col. 1

(n) ram	veruis coillart chastre motoun	}	ARIES
(n) ewe 670	oaille		OUIS MATRIX
(n) goat	cheure		CAPRA
a mastiff, dog	vn mastyn chien	}	CANIS
(n) wolf	lu		LUPUS
(n) bear 675	ours		VRSUS
(n) monkey	cynge		SIMIA

---

666 *veruis*…**669** *motoun*: These terms are grouped together, but three of the four tend to indicate a castrated ram. See AND, s.v., *vervis* (wether, castrated ram); AND, s.v., *coillart* (uncastrated ram); AND, s.v., *chatri* and DMF, s.v., *chastri* (wether, castrated animal, especially sheep); AND, s.v., *mutun* (male sheep), but DMF, s.v., *mouton1* (sheep; in particular castrated ram). In CUL Add. 8870, fol. 31ᵛ, *vervis* and *collart* are joined by a bracket and glossed as 'i. vervex, anglice vedure' (id est male sheep, in English wether), followed by *chastre* and *moton*, glossed as *aries* and *id est [aries]*. This is a rare bracketed entry in CUL Add. 8870, not noted by Baker, 'A French Vocabulary', p. 91, who does record two other bracketed entries in the section on animals, and who notes that *aries* would be the appropriate gloss only for *collart*. **670** *ouis matrix*: Literally: mother sheep. **671** *cheure capra*: Cf. fol. 148ᵛ, col. 3.

(n) small monkey	mimonet	marmuset
(n) hind	berche	a hynde
(n) buck	deyn	a buk*e*
(n) doe 680	deyme	a do
(n) marten, polecat	martrir	a fulmard
(n) polecat, marten	fouma	a wesil
(n) weasel, ermine	mustele	a whitrat
(n) hedgehog 685	heriz herison	HERINACI*US*

---

677   *mimonet marmuset*: See DMF, s.v., *maimonnet*, and Godefroy, s.v., *mainmonnet*, which take the term to indicate a kind of monkey. See also AND, s.v., *marmeset*; MED, s.v., *marmusset*; and CUL Add. 8870, fol. 31ᵛ, and Baker, 'A French Vocabulary', p. 92n54, where *mymonet* and *marmoset* are separate entries.   **678**   *berche*: Harley 219 and CUL Add. 8870, fol. 31ᵛ (Baker, 'A French Vocabulary', p. 92), record the entry *berche*, likely as a variant or error for AND, s.v., *bisse1* (hind) or its variant *biche2*.   **679**   *deyn*: AND, s.v., *deim*.   **680**   *deyme*: AND, s.v., *deime*.   **681**   *martrir…fulmard*: AND, s.v., *martre1* (marten) and MED, s.v., *fulmard* (polecat) are weasel-like animals; see also Baker, 'A French Vocabulary', p. 91n49.   **682**   *fouma*: A variant of AND, s.v., *fwyne* (polecat, marten), paired with MED, s.v., *wesel(e* (weasel; marten). CUL MS Add. 8870, fol. 31ᵛ (Baker, 'A French Vocabulary', p. 92) records a further variation: *fouvyn* (also with the gloss *wesill*).   **683**   *mustele…whitrat*: AND, s.v., *mustele*, means weasel, but MED, s.v., *whit-rat*, suggests that the ermine may be specific white-furred creature denoted.

(n) glass snake or small-worm	Noruez	a snake
(n) toad	crepaude	BUFO
(n) frog	Raine	RANA
(n) spider	eraine	ARANCA
(n) fly 690	musche	MUSCA
(n) snail	lymache	LIMAX
(n) hen	poule	a henchyken
(n) pullet	poulet	a cokerel
(n) young chicken	poucyn	a chyken

---

686 *Noruez*: Elision or corruption of *une orvez*. DMF, s.v., *orvet*, and Cotgrave, s.v., *orver*, mean snake or serpent; TLF, s.v., *orvet*, attests *orviez* (1390) and *orvez* (1581) as precursors to the Modern French term for a legless reptile whose tail is easily broken, also called a glass serpent. CUL Add. 8870, fol. 31ᵛ (Baker, 'A French Vocabulary', p. 93), adds an indefinite article: *une nornez* (with Middle English gloss *a snake*). **691** *lymache limax*: DMF, s.v., *limace*, and DMLBS, s.v., *limax*, both mean snail, but see AND, s.v., *limace* (tortoise) and *limaçon* (snail or tortoise).

693 poulet fol. 151ʳ, col. 2

(n) goose	695	ouue / snayle / oaie	AUCA
(n) young goose		gars	AUCER
(n) young goose		saison	IUUENIS AUCA
(n) gosling	700	oaiselon / ouuelet	ANCERULUS
(n) duck/duckling		ane anet	a doke
(n) swan		cine	a swan
(n) heron		herron	ARDEA
(n) crane	705	grue	GRUS

---

695 *ouue*: AND, s.v., *owei*, and DMF, s.v., *oie* (goose). **696** *snayle*: MED, s.v., *snail*, appears to be a misplaced gloss for *lymache*, above. The closest French term is DMF, s.v., *suial*, a young animal that still follows its mother. **697** *oaie*: AND, s.v., *owei* and DMF, s.v., *oie* (goose). **699** *saison*: Error for DMF, s.v., *oison* (young goose, gosling) or AND, s.v., *oiselon* (chick, young bird). CUL Add. 8870, fol. 31ᵛ (Baker, 'A French Vocabulary', p. 93) records *oayson*. **700** *oaiselon*: AND, s.v., *oiselon*. **701** *ancerulus*: DMLBS, s.v., *ansercolus*, or DuCange, s.v., *ancerulus*. CUL MS Add. 8870, fol. 31ᵛ (Baker, 'A French Vocabulary', p. 93): *ancerilus*. **702** *ane...doke*: AND, s.v., *anei* and *anetei*. The Middle English gloss in CUL Add. 8870, fol. 31ᵛ (Baker, 'A French Vocabulary', p. 93) for *anete* is 'a yong duk'.

(n) sparrow	moisson	PASSER
(n) starling	estournel	a starlynge
(n) magpie	agase	PICA
(n) jackdaw, chough	kauue	MONEDULA
(n) thrush 710	mauys	a thrusshe
(n) crow	cornaille	a crowe
(n) raven	Corber	a Rauene
(n) crow, raven	Corbelle	—
(n) lark	allouet	ALAUDA
715	alloue	
(n) thrush, blackbird	chardonet	a thrustil cok or a nosel

---

709 *kauue*: AND, s.v., *choue*. See also CUL Add. 8870, fol. 32ʳ, and Baker, 'A French Vocabulary', p. 94n78. **710** *mauys*: AND, s.v., *mauviz*. **716** *chardonet*: See DMF, s.v., *chardonnet* (goldfinch), and AND, s.v., *chardon* (linnet). CUL Add. 8870, fol. 32ʳ, records *chardenee*, with gloss *a throstulkok*. Baker, 'A French Vocabulary', p. 94, interprets the scribe's headword as 'charderiee', but in my assessment, the scribe typically uses a long *r* or 2-shaped *r*, neither of which is represented in this term, so I interpret two minims that represent an *n*. | *thrustil cok*: MED, s.v., *throstel-cok* (a male song thrush, blackbird, or mistle thrush).

(n) bat		sorischau	VESPERTILIO
(n) wren		roitel	REGULUS
(n) (gos)hawk	720	ostour	a goshauke
(n) spearhawk		esperuer	a sperhauke
(n) kite		estofle	MILUUS
(n) robin		verder	a Ruddoke
(n) tit, small bird		mosenge	a titemose
(n) snipe	725	betar	a snyte
(n) peacock		poun	PAUO
(n) ſtork		cigoigne	a storke

---

717 ...*nosel*: This gloss is 'an osel' split incorrectly (plausibly a copying or auditory error). MED, s.v., *osel(e* (blackbird). **718** *sorischau*: See AND, s.v., *chaufsoris* and *suriz*, and CUL Add. 8870, fol. 32ʳ (Baker, 'A French Vocabulary', p. 95). See also *soriz*, fol. 149ᵛ, col. 2. **721** *esperuer*: See also fol. 148ᵛ, col. 2. **722** *eſtofle*: AND, s.v., *escufle*. **723** *verder...Ruddoke*: AND, s.v., *vereder1* (wren or robin); MED, s.v., *ruddok(e* (robin redbreast). **725** *betar*: AND, s.v., *bekas* (snipe), suggests that a scribal substitution of *t* for *k* or *c* was not uncommon; cf. CUL Add. 8870, fol. 32ʳ (Baker, 'A French Vocabulary', p. 95): *betaz*.

---

723 verder fol. 151ʳ, col. 3

(n) barnacle-goose	blaret	
(n) goose	owe	—
(n) ladybird 730	paleuole	
a helmet	vn bacynet	—
(pl n) gauntlets	gancellettes de feer	gloues of plate
(n) breastplate	peitryne	a brestplate
(n) armor (esp. that covers abdomen)	pesse de mail	a paunce
(n) lance 735	gleue launce	LANCEA

---

728 *blaret*: AND s.v., *blaret*, def. 3 (barnacle-goose). CUL Add. 8870, fol. 32ʳ (Baker, 'A French Vocabulary', p. 95), glosses *blaret* with *bernak*. MED, s.v., *bernak(e* indicates a wild goose or barnacle-goose. The Bibbesworth manuscripts T, fol. 129ᵛ, and O, fol. 337ᵛ, respectively gloss *blaret* as 'a belled gos' (MED, s.v., *balled*, def. 2b, suggests a bald coot) and 'cormeraunt'; see Annie Owen, ed., *Le Traité de Walter de Bibbesworth sur la langue française* (Presses universitaires de France, 1929). | *blaret…730 paleuole*: Hoccleve brackets these three terms, without a gloss that might explain the rationale.   **730** *paleuole*: AND, s.v., *palevole* (winged insect or bird) indicates uncertainty about the varied definitions, but *ladybird* is suggested by Rita Caprini, '"Chenilles" et "coccinelles" en Gascogne', *Géolinguistique*, 19 (2019), https://journals.openedition.org/geolinguistique/1038 [accessed 22 December 2023]. See also the Introduction, p. xxvii.   **732** *gancellettes*: DMF, s.v., *gantelet*; see AND, s.v., *gant*, with variant spelling *gaunce*.   **733** *peitryne*: AND, s.v., *peitrine1*, and DMF, s.v., *poitrine*, attest uses referring to the human chest or the breastplate of a horse's harness; the related term AND, s.v., *piz1*, def. 4, attests an extension to armor.   **734** *pesse…paunce*: Literally: 'piece of mail'; see also MED, s.v., *paunce*.

(n) penknife	trencheplume	a penneknyf
(n) head of household	Menager	an housbonde
(n) housewife	menagre	a howswyf
(n) thresher 740	flaello*u*r	a thresshe*r*e
(n) cowherd	vacher	a Cowherde
(n) swineherd	porcher	a swynherde
(n) plowman	charruer	a plowman
(n) delver	faniour	a deluere
(n) ditch-digger 745	ffosseo*u*r	a dychere

---

738 *Menager…housbonde*: AND, s.v., *mesnager*; MED, s.v., *housbonde*, def. 2.
739 *menagre…howswyf*: AND, s.v., *mesnere*; MED, s.v., *hous-wif*.
740 *flaellour…thresshere*: The verbs AND, s.v., *flaeler*, DMF, s.v., *flaeller*, and MED, s.v., *threshen*, all mean to whip or scourge. MED, s.v., *thresher*, examples clarify that the noun denoted the agricultural fieldworker who separated grain from plants by threshing. The noun AND, s.v., *flaelur* seems to refer to a spear-thrower or executioner, based on the Latin glossed by its only example; see also TLF, s.v., *flageller*, def. A, for a later attestation for a thresher of wheat.
744 *faniour…deluere*: DMF, s.v., *faneur*, is one who tosses hay; MED, s.v., *delver*, is 'one who digs, a ditcher, a cultivator of fields'. This gloss is presumably closer to the latter meaning, since *dychere* glosses the next entry *ffosseour*.
745 *ffosseour…dychere*: AND, s.v., *fosseur*; DMF, s.v., *fosseur1*; MED, s.v., *dicher*.

(n) plasterer	plasterer	a daubere
(n) mower, reaper	siour	a sherere
(n) mower	facheour	a mowere
(n) male servant	varleton	a groom
(n) maidservant 750	baisellette	ANCILLA
(n) godfather	Mon parrin	PATRINUS
(n) godmother	ma marrine	MATRINA
(n) stepfather	parastre	stepfadir
(n) stepmother	marastre	stepfmodir

---

746 *plasterer…daubere*: AND, s.v., *plastreri* (one who applies plaster to walls); MED, s.v., *dauber*. **747** *siour…sherere*: See the identical entry on fol. 149ᵛ, col. 2. **751** *Mon parrin*: MS: This final folio is divided into only two columns: the first takes up a third of the folio, and the second column takes up the other two-thirds. **752** *marrine matrina*: AND, s.v., *marrene*; DMLBS, s.v., *matrinus*, def. 2b. **753** *stepfadir*: MS: *p* corrected from *f* or tall *s*.

751 Mon parrin fol. 151ᵛ, col. 1 (of 2)

(n) grandfather	755	aiel	AUUS
		grant sire	
		monseigneur	
		le grant	
(n) grandmother		beaulole	—
	760	grande dame	
(n) godson		filuoil	FILIOLUS
(n) goddaughter		filluaille	FILIOLA
(n) barley		orge	—
(n) malt		brees	BRASIUM
(n) rye	765	sigle	SILIGO
(n) vetch		vesches	—
(n) smelt		espelankes	smeltes

---

759 *beaulole…*760 *dame*: See above, fol. 148ᵛ, col. 1, where *Beaulole* is the headword and *grande dame* is the English (?) gloss.   **764** *brees brasium*: AND, s.v., *brais1*; DMLBS, s.v., *bracium*.

(n) pike, dogfish	brochie chien de meer	—
(n) ash tree	frasne	FRAXIN*US*
(n) willow tree 770	sauche	SALIX wilw
(n) boxwood tree	bochet	BUXUS beech *and* box
(n) hazel	coure	CORULUS hesil
(n) yew tree	hife	an v. tre

---

768 *brochie…meer*: DMF, s.v., *brochet*, AND, s.v., *brochete2*, and modern French *brochet* refer to the pike. For *chien de mer*, the fish list interpolated in manuscripts B and O of Bibbesworth's *Tretiz* includes *chenet*, glossed as *hundfish* (see Owen, ed., *Traité*). There seems to have been confusion of the pike and dogfish in medieval vocabularies; see Hunt, *TLL*, 2.66 and 81, s.v., *dent(r)ix* (pike), glossed as 'chevit de metir' (*sic*: chien de mer) and 'luz' (pike). See also Baker, 'A French Dictionary', p. 97n114, and AND, s.v., *chen, chenet1*. **770** *sauche*: AND, s.v., *sauz*; DMF, s.v., *sauce2*. This entry is the first of four tree terms glossed in both Latin and English. CUL Add. 8870, fol. 32ᵛ (Baker, 'A French Vocabulary', p. 97), similarly offers Latin and English glosses for most of its trees. **771** *bochet*: The spelling AND, s.v., *bochet3* (box tree) is attested only in Baker's edition of CUL Add. 8870, fol. 32ᵛ, which likewise erroneously glosses it as a beech tree: 'une bochet buxus, *anglice* beche' (Baker, 'A French Vocabulary', p. 97); see AND, s.v., *buis1* for more common spellings. Hoccleve or his source hedges bets by adding the correct tree name. Bibbesworth's *Tretiz* might provide a source for the correction *box*, which is frequently seen in *Tretiz* manuscripts (Thomas Hinton, personal correspondence); see, for example, *Tretiz*, ed. Rothwell, p. 19, line 699. See also Skeat, 'Nominale sive Verbale', p. 20. **773** *coure corulus*: AND, s.v., *coudre*; DMLBS, s.v., *corylus*. **774** *hife…tre*: AND, s.v., *hif*. The English gloss uses the single letter *v* and a punctus to evoke the sound of MED, s.v., *eu*. Cf. CUL Add. 8870, fol. 32ᵛ: vne hyf *id est* vtre (Baker, 'A French Vocabulary', p. 97).

(n) walnut tree 775	noier	AUELANA walnote tre
wipe your hands	torchez voz mains	wype yo*ur* handes
that is, and dry your hands, too	essuez vox mains	IDEM EST and drye yo*ur* handes also
wipe your eyes	terdez voz yeulx	wype yo*ur* eyen
blow your nose 780	mouchez voſtre nies	snyte yo*ur* nose
an elder tree	vn sehu	an ellir tre
it is no joke	Jl nest pas gas	it is no iape

---

775 *auelana*: DMLBS, s.v., *abellana*. CUL Add. 8870, fol. 32ᵛ, contains only the English gloss (Baker, 'A French Vocabulary', p. 97). | *tre*: MS: The two letters *tr* extend into the second column of text, between lines of the 'phrasebook'. This is the last of only 24 lines of text in this column; fol. 151ʳ contained columns of between 28–30 lines.   **778** *handes also*: MS: The word *also* is written beneath *handes*, and a line drawn to connect them at left.   **779** *terdez...eyen*: MS: A line is drawn through the middle of this entire entry.   **780** *mouchez*: AND, s.v., *mucher*.   **782** *vn...tre*: AND, s.v., *seur*; DMF, s.v., *seü*; MED, s.v., *eller*. In CUL Add. 8870, fol. 32ᵛ, this term appears between the box tree and hazel, which are in Harley 219's previous column.   **783** *gas*: AND, s.v., *gab*.

776 torchez... mains fol. 151v, col 2 (of 2)

I came for nothing else	Je ne vyns p*ur* el ⁷⁸⁵	y ca*m* for not elles
I did it unwillingly	Je le fiz enuis	y dide it maug*re* my teeth
wring the clothes	tordez les draps	wrynge the clothes
(n) the opposite	rebours	the cont*r*are
(adj) surly, hostile ⁷⁹⁰	rebours	froward
as one might say, this is an unruly churl	come len pooit dire cestui est villain rebours	this is a froward cherl
blade of a knife	lemele	a blade of a knyf

---

787 *teeth*: MS: This term appears on the line below, with an *L*-shaped line to distinguish it from the next gloss. **789** *rebours*…**790** *froward*: MS: A bracket at right joins these two entries. **790** *rebours*: DMF, s.v., *rebours*, I. adj. (surly, hostile); AND, s.v., *reburs*, attests only the adjective use of 'blunt, having lost its sharpness', with one example describing a blunt sword. **791** *come*…**792** *dire*: Presumably this phrase needed no translation. Kristol, ed., *Manières*, pp. 54–55, records a range of French insults, without glosses, but none matches this entry. See Critten, *French Lessons*, p. 142n124, on strong language and swearing in language manuals. **793** *rebours*: MS: The term *rebours* appears on a second line, followed by a horizontal slash dividing it from the English gloss; a bracket to the right connects the two lines. **794** *lemele*: MS: One blank line precedes this entry. This section has a pilcrow at the beginning of each line. This headword has an erasure of initial *A* (both *alemele* and *lemele* are attested spellings). As Sobecki, 'Handwriting', p. 12, has shown, this line and those following likely were added by Hoccleve's Privy Seal colleague Richard Priour.

my knife is rusty 795	Mon cotel est roillie	my knyf is rusty
[see note]	le corps est souz ^deinz^ lame	the body is wi*th*ynne the toumbe
since that day 800	Puissedy	syn þ*at* tyme
I am unwilling	Ie suy enuys	y am loth
I am old	Ie suy envielly	y am aged
the tree is old or aged	larbre est enviesy	the tree is old or aged

---

795 *roillie*: AND, s.v., *ruil*.   **797** *the*: MS: Above *souz* (under, beneath) is written interlinearly *deinz* (inside), likely in the same hand, perhaps to align the French more with the Middle English, though the gloss misses the joke of the body being beneath DMF, s.v., *lame1*, def. C (the tombstone). On the gloss, see Introduction, pp. lii–liv.   **800** *Puissedy…tyme*: AND, s.v., *puiscedi*. MED, s.v., *time* (n2), def. 2b(c), gives precedent for reading 'time' as 'day(s)' in certain phrases.   **801** *enuys*: AND, s.v., *enviz*, DMF, s.v., *envis1*, and Cotgrave, s.v., *envis*, record only the adverb meaning 'unwillingly'.   **802** *envielly*: AND, s.v., *enviellir*; this is the past participle form used as an adjective: grown old.   **804** : A variant for *enviely*, AND s.v., *enviezir*. The concurrence of 'y am aged' with 'the tree is old or aged' calls to mind the tree as a metaphor for the aging human body, as seen, for example in Filippo da Novara, *Les .iiij. tenz d'aage d'ome*, ed. and trans. Silvio Melani (Dipartimento di studi linguistici e letterari, Università degli studi di Padova, 2020), p. 338.

bring me my slippers 805	Baillez moy mes cafignou*n*s	take me my pynsou*n*s
this is a rented horse	Cest chiual de lowage	this is an hyred hors
while he was there	tantdyz qil y feust	While he was ther*e*

---

806 *cafignouns*: Error (or variant?) for Latin *caliga* plus diminutive French suffix; no similar term is attested in DMF or AND, but Cotgrave, s.v., *caliges*, records the usage for stockings. DMLBS, s.v., *caliga*, attests the meanings of 'footwear, esp. hose' or 'knitted stocking' that could extend to slippers. See also *chauces*, fol. 150ᵛ, col. 2. The Normandy dialect includes a similar term *kafignons*, indicating the cloven hoof of animals, in Louis du Bois, *Glossaire du patois normand* (Caen: A. Hardel, 1856), p. 203, which the anonymous press reviewer suggests may extend to 'slippers' or 'clogs'. | *pynsouns*: MS: The word extends almost into the binding of the manuscript. MED, s.v., *pinson*, is defined as a thin shoe or slipper, but some examples pair the term with a form of *sok* (sock) as if the two are synonyms, or with *shoe*, when sock or stocking might apply equally as well as 'slipper'; see also AND, s.v., *pinçun*.   **808** *hyred hors*: See Hoccleve, *Epistle of Cupid*, l. 103.   **809** *tantdyz...there*: MS: This line appears to be in lighter ink and hastily executed. It extends almost into the binding of the manuscript.

INDICES

Index of All Words Used by Hoccleve[1]

abaiez	21	alauda	31, 69
abatre	18	alia	62
abuurer	44	aliqui	17
accoler	20	alloue	69
accordance	5	allouet	69
accordement	5	aloue	31
accort	5	also	76
acheuer	23	am	78
acuere	5	amarum	45
acutus	3	amender	3
ad	3, 5	amer	33, 45
adaquare	44	amica	4
ades	3, 29, 45	amie	4
adiscere	44	amont	3
adrad	8	amourette	4
adubber	3	amplecti	20
aerder	5	ancerulus	68
afiler	5	ancilla	21, 73
afoler	7	ancillitas	22
agase	69	ancle	23, 45
aged	78	ancois	4, 44
agu	3	and	30, 45–49, 75–76
aguser	5		
aiel	74	ane	68
ains	4	anee	3
al	3	anelare	21
alaitier	31	anet	68

---

[1] Neither definite nor indefinite articles have been recorded. References are to page numbers.

anglice	17	attendre	5, 43
anientiser	5	attingenter	42
annes	15	attingere	43
annoier	16	aual	3, 44
annus	3	aualer	4
antequam	4, 44	auant	4
aperire	35	auarus	9
apparailler	4	auca	35, 68
apparare	4	aucer	68
apprendre	4	aucuns	17
approbare	23	audit	35
aprendre	44	auelana	76
aptare	41	aures	51
aranca	67	auus	74
arbre	12	bacynet	71
ardea	68	baier	20
arierisser	5	baillez	79
aries	65	baiselette	21
arouue	20	baisellette	73
arraier	4	baisselle	22
arrester	5	bake	48
arterie	58	baler	8
arteries	58	banc	61
articuli	56	bankeour	61
artificium	33	barater	20
artols	56	barette	59
arumee	20	baroun	15
assaier	4	batre	18
asselle	53	beaulole	20, 74
asselles	53	beech	75
assembler	5	beer	21
assimulari	18	belwe	63
assure	55	berche	66
atirer	4	betar	70
attaignaument	42	bittir	33
attamer	4	blade	77
atteindre	43	blamer	7
attendere	5	blancher	6

blaret	71	browez	21
blazon	53	buef	6
bobanceour	17	buer	6
bobancer	21	buette	20
bochet	75	bufo	67
bodeyns	6	buire	20
body	78	buke	66
boelt	20	bullit	20
boiaux	57	burette	20
bolengier	6, 63	butirum	20
book	30	buttokes	55
boste	21	buxus	75
boterel	6	caccare	22
botes	60	caccauit	22
bouche	52	cadere	10
bouger	6	cafignouns	79
bougre	7	cake	63
bougrenie	7	calcaria	60
bouter	16	calf	55
boviculus	6	calidi	21
box	75	calige	60
boyaux	6	calle	60
bracce	21, 59	cam	77
bracerie	21	campane	48
brachia	21, 53	canis	65
brais	21, 59	capella	59
bras	21, 53	capicium	58
brasier	21	capistrum	64
brasium	74	capra	25, 65
brees	74	captiuus	9
breis	21	caput	51
brestplate	71	caroler	8
brewe	21	cart	31
brichet	62	caste	18
brinde	64	cauilla	56
brochie	75	cerebrum	56
broilart	6	ceruel	56
brouuez	6	cest	79

cestui	77		coier	9
chaitif	9		coife	59
chalour	58		coillart	65
chanuz	40		coillons	55
chapel	59		cok	69
chaperoun	58		cokerel	67
chardonet	69		col	52
charruer	72		cold	50
chastre	65		collum	52
chatiller	22		combatre	18
chauces	60		come	77
chemise	59		coment	50
chenure	25		comparer	18, 45
cheoir	10		compasser	45
cherl	77		compasser	9
cheuestre	64		concordancia	5
cheuille	23, 45, 56		conducit	30
cheure	25, 65		confesser	9
chiche	9		congregare	5
chien	65, 75		conort	10
chier	22		conquerre	17
chiner	22		continuelment	45
chioit	22		contrare	77
chiual	79		conuoier	15
chiueux	51, 61		coquere	48
chiuille	23		cor	57
chyken	67		corbelle	69
cier	40		corber	69
cigoigne	70		cordelet	61
cine	68		cornaille	69
cineres	21		cornet	45, 59
cingere	40		corporis	51, 56
cirotece	60		corps	78
cito	3		corroucez	15
claudere	19		corsette	59
clore	19		corulus	75
clothes	77		cote	59
cocus	64		cotel	78

coucher	13	damoisele	13
couerchiefs	61	dancer	8
coure	75	dargent	62
coustees	54	daubere	73
coustre	22	de	5, 55–56, 60, 71, 75, 79
cousture	22		
cousturer	22	dealbare	6
coutes	53	debate	20
cowherde	72	decalciare	23
crainant	8	dechaucier	23
craindre	7	decipere	42, 49
crains	8	deffaire	5
crainte	8	deficit	46
craticula	63	deius	3, 44
cremeteus	8	deinz	78
cremeur	8	delier	11
cremir	7	deligare	11
cremuz	8	deluere	72
crepare	22	demesner	15
crepaude	67	demorer	5
creuer	22	dens	52
crines	51	dentes	52
croler	8	deponere	16, 42
crooke	63	deporter	9
croper	64	deridere	11
crowe	69	derisio	11
cubiti	53	derision	11
cuel	55	des	15
cuer	57	descendere	4
cueure	22	descendre	4
culer	64	dessus	3
culpare	7	deuiare	12
culus	55	deuorare	10
cupa	62	deuorer	10
cupe	62	deyme	66
cuprum	22	deyn	66
cynge	65	dide	77
dame	20, 74	digiti	53

diligere	45	enombrer	35
dimittere	46	enseigner	4
dire	77	enterine	12
do	50, 66	entiere	12
docere	4, 44	entrailles	6
dois	53	enuis	77
doke	68	enuis	47
dokes	15	enuoier	17
dolet	23	enuys	78
domicella	13	envielly	78
dormis	23	enviesy	78
dors	23, 54	epar	26, 57
dorsum	23, 54	equales	35
dos	23	equiuoca	44
doseour	61	equos	44
doublet	60	eraine	67
doun	18	erbuse	12
douter	10	esbatement	13
draps	77	esbatre	18, 45
drye	76	escharn	11
dubitare	10	escharnir	11
ducere	15	eschauder	25
duelt	23	Escurer	40
dychere	72	espandre	11
egales	35	esparnir	23
egge	49	espaules	52
eiectice	27	espelankes	74
el	77	espernir	23
elles	77	esperuer	23, 70
ellir	76	espingles	24, 61
embracer	20	espoentez	8
emendare	3	esporons	60
empoigner	24	esprouer	23
enchantour	12	espuisent	36
endurer	9	esracher	11
enfementer	12	essartir	11
enfrim	9	essuer	24
englouter	10	essuez	76

est	28–29, 76–78	fauces	52
estaint	24	faut	46
estamyn	63	fauxine	25
estanche	24	faxwax	52
estancher	24	faye	26
estendre	11	feer	71
estirper	11	fel	57
estofle	70	fendre	27
estournel	69	fendure	27
estreim	11	fer	27
estreine	24	ferai	26
estruz	64	fererai	26
et	44–50, 62	ferir	19
euellere	11	fermer	19
exclamare	22	ferrai	26
expandere	11	ferrare	25
expectare	43	ferraui	26
exstinguit	24	ferrer	25
extransuerso	42	fetare	17
eyen	76	fetens	38
fac	26	fetere	38
faceoun	25	fetes	36
facheour	73	fetet	36
faciam	26	fetor	36
factura	25	feust	79
fade	47	fforuoier	12
fadith	47	ffosseour	72
fai	26	ffourner	6
faim	26	fibule	34
fait	50	fiel	57
faites	50	fiens	26
falsitas	25	fil	13
fames	26	filet	13
faniour	72	filiol	13
faren	50	filiola	13, 74
fast	48	filiole	13
fat	63	filiolus	13, 74
fateras	26	fillette	13

filluaille	74	founde	27
filum	13	founder	27
filuoil	74	fourner	*see ffourner*
fimus	26	foye	57
findere	27	frangere	38
finer	46	frangunt	36
finire	23	fraper	19
fiola	20	frasne	75
fissure	27	fraxinus	75
fist	24	frein	64
fistula	12	frenum	64
fiz	77	fretele	12
flaeller	25	friande	14
flaellour	72	froit	50
flagellare	25	frons	51
flairer	12	front	51
flanks	54	froward	77
fleint	47	fryyngpanne	62
flenir	25	fuet	27
fleshhooke	63	fulmard	66
fleume	58	fume	26
flogot	12	fumosus	46
fluhute	12	fumous	46
fluir	47	fumus	26
fodere	25	fundare	27
fol	10	fundit	27
folde	24	fust	12, 27
fondu	34	fyste	17, 43
for	77	gaigner	28
foramen	16	gainer	28
forsake	46	gale	19
forscrier	22	gale	13
forsener	46	galous	19
foruoier	*see fforuoier*	gancellettes	71
fosseour	*see ffosseour*	gans	60
fouet	27	garet	55
fouir	25	garnir	47
fouma	66	gars	68

gas	76	hanches	55
gaudere	45	handes	76
genoilles	55	hanselle	24
genua	55	hauriens	37
giser	13	haurire	38
glade	29	hauriunt	36
gleue	71	he	79
gloues	71	hefre	64
go	46	hemp	25
gobre	62	henchyken	67
gorgat	56	here	30
gorge	13, 52	heresie	7
gorget	13, 56	heresis	7
goshauke	70	heretic	7
goulper	10	hereticus	7
goute	16	herinacius	66
graille	63	herison	66
graine	16	heriz	66
grand	20	herron	68
grande	74	hesil	75
grant	50, 74	hetier	29
grater	28	heuy	37
gray	44	Hic	44
grece	41	hife	75
greignour	29	hirid	31
greindre	29	hirsutus	44
gret	50	hodie	29
gristel	52	homme	35
groom	73	homo	35
grownden	32	honir	7
grue	68	hoor	40
grus	68	hopelande	59
grype	24	hora	30
guerres	47	horn	45
guinher	28	hors	79
guopil	19	hostium	29
guttur	13, 52	hous	21
hamme	55	housbonde	72

how	50	ita	34
howswyf	72	iunctae	53
hui	29	iungere	29
humani	51	iuuenis	68
humours	58	ja	see ia
huys	29	je	see ie
hynde	66	jl	see il
hyred	79	joeuece	64
ia, ja	5, 16, 29, 47	jontes	29
iacere	13	jupoun	59
iactare	18	kakele	29
iam	47	kaqueter	29
iambe	55	kauue	69
iambes	55	keuue	63
iape	76	knede	38, 48
iapere	26	knyf	77–78
id	28–29	kuttynge	49
idem	46, 54, 76	la	56, 58
ie, je	77–78	labia	30, 52
ietter	18	lactare	31
ignis	27	laidanger	14
il, jl	50, 76	lame	78
ille	36	lancea	71
in	50	langue	52
incantator	12	larbre	78
incendium	21	las	14
inferius	3	laskes	54
inferre	18	latrare	20
innuere	28	laudat	30
integra	12	launce	71
Interiora	56	laus	14, 30
iocus	13	lechefryt	62
ioindre	29	lechierres	14
iointes	53	lede	14
iouues	52	lemele	77
iratus	15	len	35, 77
is	50, 76–79	lene	55
it	50, 76–77	lentille	15

lepararius	30	luere	45
lepus	30	lupus	30, 65
leschyn	54	lymache	67
leuerer	30	ma	51–53, 55–56, 73
leure	30		
leuure	30	madre	62
liens	13	mahutes	53
lier	31	mail	71
lieures	30, 52	maindre	31
liez	31	mains	53, 76
ligacions	13	maior	29
ligamina	13	mais	4
ligare	31	make	48
ligatures	13	makerellefe	31
ligatus	31	makereumas	31
lignum	12, 27	malencolie	58
likerous	14	mamelles	54
limax	67	mamille	54
lingua	52	mander	17
liripipium	59	manere	31
liure	30	mantel	60
loenge	14, 30	manus	53
loier	14	marastre	73
loke	48	mare	32
longitudo	15	marit	15
longuesce	15	maritus	15
longum	47	marmuset	66
longure	15	marri	15
loqui	48	marrine	73
los	14, 30	marrir	12
loth	78	marrite	57
loue	33	martrir	66
louue	30	maser	62
lowage	79	mastyn	65
lowez	31	mater	32
lu	30, 65	matrina	73
lucrare	28	matrix	65
ludere	18, 45	maugre	77

mauys	69	moel	31
me	55, 79	moeuer	6
mea	51–56	moilee	32
medicus	33	moisson	69
medulla	32	moker	11
mee	51–55	mokerie	11
meer	32, 75	mokeson	11
mei	51–53, 55–56	molais	63
		mole	32
melius	31	molle	32
membrorum	51	molten	34
menager	72	molu	32
menagre	72	mon	51–56, 73, 78
mener	15	monedula	69
menour	31	monseigneur	74
menton	52	mosenge	70
mentum	52	motoun	65
merite	14	mouchez	76
mes	51–56, 79	mouelle	32
mestier	33	mouere	6
mestir	33	mowere	73
meta	32	moy	79
mete	15	mue	32
meum	51–54	muet	33
meus	51, 54–56	mulierum	54
meute	32	multum	47
midryfe	57	munire	47
miendre	31	mus	40
miere	32	musart	10
miluus	70	musca	43, 67
mimonet	66	musche	67
minus	31	mustele	66
mire	33	mutat	33
mirer	15, 33	mutus	32
mist	6, 21	my	52, 54–55, 77–79
mitaynes	60		
mittere	17	mye	16
moeille	32	naire	34

naistre	34	nuces	33
nares	52	nudus	34
narins	52	nues	34
nasci	34	nunquam	47
nasus	51	nupcie	34
natare	34	nuyser	16
natiuus	33	nuz	34
naue	31	oaie	68
nauis	33	oaille	65
ne	77	oaiselon	68
necesse	33	obligacions	14
neif	33	obumbrare	35
nerfs	58	ocree	60
nerui	58	oculi	51
nest	76	oculis	28
nief	33	oculus	34
nient	16	odorabis	49
nies	51, 76	odorer	12
nix	33	odorere	12
no	76	oeil	34
nocere	16	of	71, 77
noces	34	oil	34
noeaus	34	oint	34
noef	33	old	78
noes	33	ombrer	35
noier	76	on	35
noiez	34	operari	35
noif	33	oportet	46
nomina	51	optare	28
non	16, 29, 47	or	69, 78
non	16	orailler	35
noruez	67	orde	14
nose	76	ore	5
nosel	69	oreilles	51
not	77	orge	74
nouem	33	os	52, 54
now	29	ossa	54
nubes	34	ostour	70

ot	35	patiser	6
ou	50	patria	37
oueles	35	patrinus	73
ouerir	35	paume	53
ouerthwerte	42	paunce	71
ouis	65	pauo	70
ours	65	pauor	8
ouster	16, 42	pax	37
ouue	35, 68	pece	62
ouuelet	68	pecia	62
ouurir	35	pecient	36
owe	71	pecier	38
paelle	62	pecten	55
paijs	37	pectus	53
paille	11	pedens	38
paire	60	pedere	38
pais	37	pedes	56
paistre	38	pedis	56
paix	37	peiant	38
paleuole	71	peire	38
palma	53	peitryne	71
palpabis	49	pel	58
palpebre	51	pellis	58
paour	8	penneknyf	72
paourous	8	penser	45
parastre	73	pentys	27
parcere	23	penyl	55
parebit	37	percer	16
parmy	44	percuciam	26
parra	37	percute	27
parrin	73	percutere	19, 42, 49
parua	12	perforare	16
paruus	27	perimplere	44
pas	16, 76	pertuser	16
pascere	38	pertuz	16
passer	69	pesant	37
patella	62	pesse	71
pati	9	pestier	38, 48

pestour	6		poule	67
petit	6		poulet	67
peu	36		poun	70
Peus	36		pound	30
pica	69		praesens	5
pie	56		premium	14
pies	56		present	5
pilioun	59		presentement	5
pilius	59		priuee	47
pilwer	35		pronuba	31
pin	45		prosmes	16
pisa	37		proximi	16
pissa	37		puant	38
pistor	6, 63		pugnare	18
pistrire	38, 48		pui	36
plane	56		puir	38
planta	56		puisant	37
plasterer	73		puiser	38
plate	71		puissant	37
plier	24		puissedy	78
plowman	72		puissent	36
poign	24		puit	36
poigner	24		pulmo	57
point	16		pulmoun	57
pois	37		pulsare	48
poisant	37		pungere	24
poitrine	53		pur	61, 77
pollex	37		purpoint	60
pompator	17		pus	36
ponderans	37		pyn	23
pondus	37		pynnes	24
pooit	77		pynsouns	79
porcher	72		qe	50
posser	37		qil	79
potens	36–37		quarreau	61
potestas	36		quatre	58
pouche	58		quir	48
poucyn	67		quir	38

quisiner	64	reumaticus	20
quisshyn	61	reynes	57
quysses	55	rien	16
radere	39	rigbon	54
radius	48	riuoli	39
raier	39	roigne	19, 39
raine	67	roignous	19
ramsiaux	38	roillie	78
ramunculi	38	roitel	70
rana	67	rotunda	62
rapere	39	rouger	39
raucus	20	rounces	39
rauene	69	ruddoke	70
rauerder	39	ruer	18
rauoier	39	ruissiaux	39
raye	39, 48	rusty	78
rebours	77	sachier	19, 39
recognoistre	9	sain	34, 41
recognoscere	9, 50	saintes	48
redoubter	10	saison	68
reed	39	salix	75
regehir	9	sanc	58
regnart	19	sancte	48
regreter	28	sancti	48
regulus	70	sanis	48
rehetier	29	sanus	48
reis	14	sarrer	48
reiteal	60	sarrer	39
remirer	15	sauche	75
renes	57	savon	41
reprendre	14	sawe	40
reprobare	14	scabellum	40
reprouer	14	scabies	19, 39
rere	39	scabiosus	19
reseier	5	scalde	25
resoluer	11	scalpere	28
ressembler	18	scelle	40, 62
retia	14	scherere	41

scies	49	snyte	70, 76
scindere	40	soeffrer	45
scintilla	20	soiourer	40
score	39, 48	soliers	60
se	40	solis	48
secree	47	soluere	46
secuntur	44	sone	29
sedibitur	41	soner	48
seem	22	sope	41
sehu	76	sorischau	70
sentiras	49	soriz	40
separare	40	sot	10
sequi	41	sotulares	60
serare	39	souffrer	9
serrez	41	sourcier	10
sesbatre	46	souz	78
set	4	sowe	64
sharp	49	spatule	52
sherere	73	speculari	15, 33
sheres	41	sperhauke	23, 70
shoure	40	spernere	23
si	40–41	splen	57
sic	41	starlynge	69
siel	63	stepfadir	73
sieu	41	stepfmodir	73
sigle	74	stiropes	64
signer	40	stomac	57
siligo	74	stomacus	57
simia	65	stool	62
simulare	45	storke	70
siour	41, 73	stramen	11
sire	74	streynour	63
siselles	41	stryke	48
situla	63	stultus	10
slinge	27	stupefactus	21
smeltes	74	submersus	34
snake	67	sudare	41
snayle	68	suer	41

suere	22	tendere	43
sufflet	63	tendre	43
suir	41	tendroun	52
sunt	54	tenelles	63
superbus	46	terdez	76
supercilia	51	tergere	24, 49
superius	3	teste	51
surcilles	51	testiculi	55
surcilz	51	tetes	54
suy	78	þat	78
swan	68	there	79
swynherde	72	this	77, 79
sydes	54	thresshere	72
Sye	40	thretebolle	56
syn	78	thrusshe	69
tabard	59	thrustil	69
table	61	thyghes	55
tacere	9	thyng	30
tailler	41	tibie	55
taillour	22	tikele	22
taindre	43	timere	7
taiser	9	timidus	8
take	79	tingere	43
taloun	56	tipet	45
talus	56	tiphielet	12
talwhe	41	tirer	19
tame	47	titemose	70
tantdyz	79	to	5, 18, 20–22, 24–25, 29, 33, 38–40, 42–43, 47–49
tarde	47		
tasse	62		
tassete	58		
teeth	77	toga	59
temperies	49	toiller	41
temps	49	toller	42
temptare	4	tollir	16
tempus	47, 49	tondere	43
tena	59	tondre	43
tenant	9	tonges	63

torcher	42, 49	vanter	21
torchez	76	vantour	17
tordez	77	varleton	73
tortir	42, 49	vbi	50
tost	45	vel	9, 50
toumbe	78	veluz	44
trahere	19, 39	vendon	52
trainer	42	vene	58
traire	39	vener	17
tramettre	17	venter	54
transglouter	10	ventre	54
trauers	42	vepres	39
trauerser	42	ver	44
tre	75–76	verba	44
tree	78	verberare	18
tremeler	49	verder	70
tremere	49	veretrum	54
trenchant	3, 49	vernus	44
trencheplume	72	verre	62
tresbucher	10	verser	43
trestle	62	vertere	43
treu	16	veruis	65
tripes	63	vesches	74
troipie	63	vesica	58
trop	9	vespertilio	70
truye	64	vesser	17, 43
tu	36, 49	vessie	58
tubbe	63	veynes	58
turpis	14	viande	15
tyme	78	vigere	22
umbrare	35	villain	77
v	75	vincere	17
vacher	72	virescere	39
vado	43	viscera	6, 57
vaginare	28	vit	54
vaincre	17	vitrum	62
vair	44	vix	47
vais	43	vmbelicus	54

vmbril	54	wet	32
vndo	5	wexe	39
vngles	53	what	50
vngues	53	while	79
vns	17	whippe	27
voisins	16	whitrat	66
vole	43	wilw	75
vostre	76	withynne	78
vouer	50	wood	46
vouere	50	wortes	29
vous	50	wrynge	42, 49, 77
vox	76	wrythe	49
voz	76	wype	76
vrsus	65	y	77–79
vulpes	19	ye	50
vyns	77	yendrois	3
walnote	76	yeulx	76
was	79	yeux	51
welke	25, 47	ymmo	44
welkith	47	yolke	32
wesil	66	your	76

Alphabetic List of French Words with Their Equivalents

a	ad	amer	diligere
a present	ad praesens	amer	loue, to
a trauers	extransuerso	amie	amica
abaiez	stupefactus	amont	superius
abatre	caste doun, to	amourette	amica
abuurer	adaquare equos	an	annus
		ancois	antequam
abuurer	perimplere ... equos	ancois	antequam
		ancois	ymmo
accoler	amplecti	ane anet	doke, a
accordance	concordancia	anee	annus
accordement	concordancia	anientiser	vndo, to
accort	concordancia	annes	dokes mete
acheuer	finire	annoier	nocere
ades	cito	apparailler	apparare
ades	continuelment	apprendre	docere
ades	now	aprendre	adiscere
ades	sone	aprendre	docere
ades	tost	arbre	lignum
adubber	emendare	arbre, l'	tree, the
aerder	congregare	arierisser	vndo, to
afiler	acuere	arouue	raucus
afoler	culpare	arraier	apparare
agase	pica	arrester	attendere
Agu	acutus	arteries, les	arterie
aguser	acuere	artols	articuli
aiel	auus	arumee	reumaticus
ains	set	assaier	temptare
al	ad	asselles	asselle
alaitier	lactare	assembler	congregare
alloue	alauda	assure, le	calf, the
allouet	alauda	atirer	apparare
aloue	alauda	attaignaument	attingenter
amender	emendare	attamer	temptare
amer	amarum	atteindre	attingere
amer	bittir	attendre	attendere

attendre	expectare	bouger	mouere
au	ad	bougre	hereticus
aual	deius	bougrenie	heresis
aual	inferius	bouter	deponere
aual	parmy	boyaux	viscera
aualer	descendere	bracerie	brewe hous, a
auant	antequam	brais	bracce
aucuns	aliqui	brais, les	bracce
baier	latrare	bras	brachia
baillez moy	take me	bras	brachia
mes	my	brasier	incendium
cafignouns	pynsouns	brees	brasium
baiselette	ancilla	breis	cineres calidi
baisellette	ancilla	brichet, vn	trestle, a
baisselle	ancillitas	brinde, vne	frenum
barater	debate, to	broilart	mist
barette, vn	tena	brouuez	mist
baroun	maritus	browez	mist
batre	verberare	buer	dealbare
beaulole	grand dame	buette	scintilla
beer	anelare	buire	butirum
berche	hynde, a	burette	fiola
betar	snyte, a	crains	adrad
blamer	culpare	cafignouns	pynsouns
blancher	dealbare	cake, vn	tubbe, a
bobanceour	pompator	ceruel, le	cerebrum
bobancer	boste, to	cest	this is
bochet	beech	cestui est	this is
bochet	box	chaitif	auarus
bochet	buxus	chaitif	captiuus
bodeyns	viscera	chanuz	hoor
boelt	bullit	chapel, vn	capella
boiaux, les	viscera	chaperoun, vn	capicium
bolengier	pistor	chardonet	nosel, a
bolengier	pistor	chardonet	thrustil cok, a
boterel	boviculus	charruer	plowman, a
botes	ocree	chastre	aries
bouche	os	chatiller	tikele, to

chauces	calige	conquerre	vincere
chenure	hemp	conuoier	ducere
cheoir	cadere	corber	Rauene, a
cheuestre, vn	capistrum	cornaille	crowe, a
cheuille	pin, a	cornet	horn, an
cheuille	ancle, an	cornet	tipet, a
cheuille	cauilla	cornet, vn	liripipium
cheure	capra	corps, le	body, the
cheure	capra	corroucez	iratus
chiche	auarus	cotel	knyf
chiche	captiuus	coucher	iacere
chien	canis	coure	corulus
chier	caccare	coure	hesil
chiner	vigere	coustees	sydes
chioit	caccauit	coustre	suere
chiual	hors, an	cousture	seem, a
chiueux	crines	cousturer	taillour, a
chiuille	pyn, a	coutes	cubiti
cier	scindere	crainant	timidus
cigoigne	storke, a	craindre	timere
cine	swan, a	crainte	pauor
clore	claudere	crainte	pauor
coier	tacere	cremeteus	timidus
coillart	aries	cremeur	pauor
coillons	testiculi	cremeur	pauor
col	collum	cremir	timere
combatre	inferre	cremuz	adrad
combatre	pugnare	crepaude	bufo
coment faites vous	how faren ye	creuer	crepare
		crooke, vn	fleshhooke, a
comparer	assimulari	cuel	culus
comparer	simulare et luere	cuer, le	cor
		cueure	cuprum
compasser	pati	culer, vn	croper, a
compasser	soeffrer, penser	cupe, vne	cupa
		cynge	simia
confesser	recognoscere	damoisele	domicella
conort	stultus	de ia ore	ad praesens

de lowage	hyred	enuis	maugre my teeth
dechaucier	decalciare		
deffaire	vndo, to	enuis	tarde et vix
deius	inferius	enuoier	mittere
delier	deligare	enuys	loth
demesner	ducere	enviesy	aged
demorer	attendere	enviesy	old
dens	dentes	eraine	aranca
deporter	pati	erbuse	incantator
derision	derisio	esbatement	iocus
descendre	descendere	esbatre	ludere
dessus	superius	esbatre	ludere, gaudere
deuorer	deuorare		
deyme	do, a	escharn	derisio
deyn	buke, a	escharnir	deridere
dois	digiti	eschauder	scalde, to
dors	dormis	eschyn, l'	rigbon, the
dors	meum dorsum	escurer	shoure, to
dos	dorsum	espandre	expandere
douter	dubitare	esparnir	parcere
draps, les	clothes, the	espaules	spatule
duelt	dolet	espelankes	smeltes
egales	equales	espernir	spernere
eiectice	pentys, a	esperuer	sperhauke, a
embracer	amplecti	esperuer	sperhauke, a
empoigner	grype, to	espingles	pynnes
enchantour	incantator	espoentez	adrad
endurer	pati	esporons	calcaria
enfementer	incantator	esprouer	approbare
enfrim	auarus	espuisent	hauriunt
enfrim	captiuus	esracher	euellere
englouter	deuorare	essartir	euellere
enombrer	obumbrare	essuer	tergere
enseigner	docere	essuez	drye your handes,
enterine	integra	vox	wype your handes
entiere	integra	mains	
entrailles	viscera		
enuielly	aged	estaint	exstinguit

estamyn, vn	streynour, a	filluaille	filiola
estancher	estanche, to	filuoil	filiolus
estendre	expandere	finer	soluere,
estirper	euellere		dimittere
estofle	miluus	flaeller	flagellare
estournel	starlynge, a	flaellour	thresshere, a
estreim	stramen	flairer	odorere
estreine	hanselle	flanks	laskes
estruz	stiropes	fleint	fadith
faceoun	factura	fleint	welkith
facheour	mowere, a	flenir	welke, to
fai	fac	flogot	parua fistula
faim	fames	fluhute	parua fistula
faniour	deluere, a	fluir	fade, to
fateras	iapere, a	fluir	welke, to
faut	deficit	fol	stultus
faut	oportet	fondu	molten
fauxine	falsitas	forscrier	exclamare
faye	epar	forsener	forsake and
fendre	findere		go wood
fendure	fissure	foruoier	*see fforuoier*
fer	percute	fosseour	*see ffoseour*
ferai	faciam	fouet	whippe, a
fererai	percuciam	fouir	fodere
ferir	percutere	fouma	wesil, a
fermer	claudere	founde	fundit
ferrai	ferraui	founde	slinge, a
ferrer	ferrare	founder	fundare
fforuoier	deuiare	fourner	see ffourner
ffosseour	dychere, a	foye, le	epar
ffourner	pistor	fraper	percutere
fiel, le	fel	frasne	fraxinus
fiens	fimus	frein, vn	frenum
fil	filum	fretele	fistula
filet	filum	friande	likerous
filiol	filiolus	front	frons
filiole	filiola	fuet	paruus ignis
fillette	domicella	fume	fumus

fumous	fumosus	hanches	buttokes
fumous	superbus	heresie	heresis
fust	lignum	heretic	hereticus
fust	lignum	herison	herinacius
gaigner	lucrare	heriz	herinacius
gainer	vaginare	herron	ardea
gale	iocus	hetier	glade, to
gale	scabies	hife	v. tre, an
galous	scabiosus	homme	homo
gancellettes de feer	gloues of plate	honir	culpare
gans	cirotece	hopelande, vne	toga
garet de ma iambe, le	hamme, the	hui	hodie
		huys	hostium
garnir	munire	ia	now, sone
gars	aucer	ia rien	see pas
gas	iape	iambes	tibie
genoilles	genua	ietter	iactare
giser	iacere	il fait grant froit	it is gret cold
gleue	lancea		
gobre, vn	pecia rotunda	il nest pas gas	it is no iape
gorgat, le	threbolle	ioindre	iungere
gorge	guttur	iointes	iunctae
gorget	guttur	iouues	fauces
gorget, le	threbolle	ja	non
goulper	deuorare	ja non	nunquam et iam
goute / graine	non		
graille, vne	craticula	je le fiz enuis	y dide it maugre my teeth
graine	see goute		
grant sire	auus		
grater	scalpere	je ne vyns pur el	y cam for not elles
greindre	maior		
grue	grus	je suy enuys	y am loth
guerres	longum tempus, multum	je suy envielly	y am aged
		joeuece	hefre, a
		jontes	wortes
guinher	oculis innuere	kaqueter	kakele, to
guopil	vulpes	kauue	monedula

keuue, vne	fat, a	louue	laudat
laidanger	reprobare	lowez	hirid
lame	toumbe, the	lu	lupus
langue	lingua	lymache	limax
larbre est	the tree is	madre, vn	maser, a
enviesy	old or aged	Maindre	manere
las	retia	mains	manus
launce	lancea	mais	set
le corps est	the body is	makerellefe	pronuba
souz deinz	withynne	Makereumas	pronuba
lame	the toumbe	mamelles	mamille
le grant	auus	mander	mittere
lechefryt	fryyngpanne	marastre	stepfmodir
lechierres	likerous	marit	maritus
lede	turpis	marri	iratus
lemele	blade of a	marrine	matrina
	knyf	marrir	deuiare
len	homo	marrite, le	midryfe
lentille	dokes mete	martrir	fulmard, a
leuerer	lepararius	mastyn, vn	canis
leure	here thyng	mauys	thrusshe, a
leure	hora	meer	mare
leuure	lepus	menager	housbonde, an
liens	ligamina	menagre	howswyf, a
lier	ligare	mener	ducere
lieures	labia	menour	minus
liez	ligatus	menton	mentum
ligacions	ligamina	merite	premium
ligatures	ligamina	mestier	artificium
liure	book, a	mestir	necesse
liure	pound, a	meute	meta
loenge	laus	miendre	melius
loenge	laus	miere	mater
loier	premium	mimonet	marmuset
longuesce	longitudo	mire	medicus
longure	longitudo	mirer	speculari
los	laus	mirer	speculari
louue	conducit	moeille	yolke, a

moel	cart naue, a	noif	nix
moeuer	mouere	non / nient	non
moilee	wet	noruez	snake, a
moisson	passer	nues	nubes
moker	deridere	nuyser	nocere
mokerie	derisio	nuz	nudus
mokeson	derisio	oaie	herinacius
molais	tonges	oaille	ouis matrix
mole	molle	oaiselon	ancerulus
molu	grownden	obligacions	ligamina
mon cotel	my knyf	odorer	odorere
est roillie	is rusty	oeil	oculus
monseigneur	auus	oil	oculus
mosenge	titemose, a	oint	molten
motoun	aries	ombrer	umbrare
mouchez	snyte	on	homo
vostre nies	your nose	orailler	pilwer, a
mouelle	medulla	orde	turpis
mue	mutus	oreilles	aures
muet	mutat	os	ossa
musart	stultus	ostour	goshauke, a
musche	musca	ot	audit
mustele	whitrat, a	ou	in, vbi, vel
naire	natare	oueles	equales
naistre	nasci	ouerir	operari
narins	nares	ours	vrsus
neif	natiuus	ouster	deponere
nerfs, les	nerui	ouster	deponere
nief	nauis	ouue	auca
nient	*see non*	ouuelet	ancerulus
nies	nasus	ouurir	aperire
noces	nupcie	paelle, vne	patella
noeaus	fibule	paijs	patria
noef	nouem	paille	stramen
noes	nuces	pais	pissa
noier	auelana	paistre	pascere
noier	walnote tre	paix	pax
noiez	submersus	paour	pauor

108   *Hoccleve's Trilingual Glossary*

paourous	timidus	poitrine	pectus
parastre	stepfadir	porcher	swynherde, a
parra	parebit	posser	pollex
parrin	patrinus	poucyn	chyken, a
pas / ia rien	non	poule	hen chyken, a
patiser	pistor	poulet	cokerel, a
paume	palma	poun	pauo
pecient	frangunt	presentement	ad praesens
pecier	frangere	priuee	secree
peiant	pedens	priuee	tame
peire	pedere	prosmes	proximi
peitryne	brestplate, a	puant	fetens
pel, la	pellis	pui	fetor
penyl	pecten	puir	fetere
percer	perforare	puisant	hauriens
pertuser	perforare	puiser	haurire
pertuz	foramen	puissant	potens
pesant	heuy	puissedy	syn þat tyme
pesse de mail	paunce, a	puissent	hauriunt
pestier	bake, to	puit	ille fetet
pestier	knede, to	pulmoun, le	pulmo
pestier	knede, to	pus	tu fetes
pestour	pistor	qe faites vous	what do ye
petit buef	boviculus	quarreau, vn	a quisshyn, a
peu	potestas	quir	pistrire
Peus	potens	quir	coquere
pies	pedes	quir pestier	pistrire
pilioun, vn	pilius	quisiner	cocus
plane de mon pie, la	planta mei pedis	quysses	thyghes
		raier	score, to
plasterer	daubere, a	raine	rana
plier	folde, to	ramsiaux	ramunculi
poign	fist, a	rauerder	virescere
poigner	pungere	4rauoier	rapere
point / mye	non	raye	radius solis
pois	pisa	raye	score, a
pois	pondus	raye	stryke, a
poisant	ponderans	rebours	contrare, the;

	froward	savon	sope
recognoistre	recognoscere	scelle	scabellum
redoubter	dubitare	scelle, vn	stool, a
regehir	recognoscere	se	si
regnart	vulpes	sehu, vn	ellir tre, an
regreter	optare	sentiras	*see tu sentiras*
rehetier	glade, to	serrez	sedibitur
reis	retia	sesbatre	ludere
reiteal, vn	a calle	sesbatre	gaudere
remirer	speculari	si	sic
reprendre	reprobare	siel, vn	situla
reprouer	reprobare	sieu	talwhe
rere	radere	sigle	siligo
reseier	attendere	signer	cingere
resoluer	deligare	siour	scherere, a;
ressembler	assimulari		sherere, a
reynes, les	renes	siselles	sheres
roigne	scabies	snayle	auca
roigne	scabies	soiourer	separare
roignous	scabiosus	soliers	sotulares
roillie	rusty	soner	loqui
roitel	regulus	soner	pulsare
rouger	wexe reed, to	sorischau	vespertilio
rounces	vepres	soriz	mus
ruer	iactare	sot	stultus
ruissiaux	riuoli	souffrer	pati
sachier	trahere	sourcier	dubitare
sain	grece	splen, le	splen
sain	molten	stomac, le	stomacus
saintes	campane	suer	sudare
saintes	sancte	sufflet, vn	belwe, a
saison	auca iuuenis	suir	sequi
sanis	sancti	surcilles	supercilia
sanis	sanus et	surcilz	palpebre
sarrer	make fast, to	Sye	sawe, a
sarrer	serare	tailler	aptare
sarrer	loke, to	taindre	tingere
sauche	salix, wilw	taiser	tacere

taloun	talus		kuttynge; sharp
tantdyz qil y feust	While he was there	trencheplume	penneknyf, a
tasse dargent	pece	tresbucher	cadere
tassete	pouche, a	treu	foramen
temps	temperies	troipie, vn	tripes
temps	tempus	trop tenant	auarus, captiuus
tenant	*see* trop tenant		
tendre	tendere	truye, vne	sowe, a
tendroun	gristel	tu sentiras	odorabis, palpabis, scies
tenelles	tonges		
terdez voz yeulx	wype your eyen	vacher	cowherde, a
teste	caput	vaincre	vincere
tetes	mamille mulierum	vair	gray
		vais	vado
tiphielet	fistula	vanter	boste, to
tirer	trahere	vantour	pompator
toller	deponere	varleton	groom, a
tollir	deponere	veluz	hirsutus
tondre	tondere	vendon, le	faxwax, the
torcher	percutere	vener	fetare
torcher	percutere	vener	fyste
torcher	tergere	ventre	venter
torchez voz mains	wype your handes	ver	vernus
		verder	ruddoke, a
tordez les draps	wrynge the clothes	verre, vn	vitrum
		verser	vertere
tortir	wrynge, to; wrythe, to	veruis	aries
		vesser	fetare; fyste; fyste, to
trainer	decipere		
traire	trahere	vessie, la	vesica
tramettre	mittere	veynes	vene
transglouter	deuorare	viande des	dokes mete
trauerser	ouerthwerte	villain	cherl
tremeler	decipere	vit	veretrum
tremeler	tremere	vmbril	vmbelicus
trenchant	acutus; egge;	vngles	vngues

vns	aliqui	vouer	vouere
voisins	proximi	yendrois	cito
vole	musca	yeux	oculi
vouer	recognoscere		

French Words without Translation

bacynet, vn
baler
banc, vn
bankeour, vn
beaulole
blaret
blazon
brochie
caroler
chalour
chemise, vne
chien de meer
coife, vne
corbelle
cordelet pur chiueux, vn
corsette, vn
cote, vne
couerchiefs
croler
dancer
doseour, vn
doublet, vn

espingles
fleume
grande dame
greignour
humours, les quatre
Jupoun, vn
lene
mahutes
malencolie
mantel, vn
orge
owe
paire de mitaynes, vne
paleuole
purpoint, vn
sachier
sanc
tabard, vn
table, vn
toiller
vesches

Latin Words Used for Translation

Latin			
acuere	afiler		coillart,
acuere	aguser		motoun,
acutus	Agu		veruis
acutus	trenchant	arterie	arteries, les
ad	a, al, au	articuli	artols
ad praesens	a present, de ia ore, presentement	artificium	mestier
		asselle	asselles
		assimulari	comparer, ressembler
adaquare equos	abuurer		
adiscere	aprendre	attendere	arrester, attendre, demorer, reseier
alauda	alloue, allouet, aloue		
aliqui	aucuns, vns	attingenter	attaignaument
amarum	amer	attingere	atteindre
amica	amie, amourette	auarus	chaitif, chiche, enfrim, trop tenant
amplecti	accoler, embracer		
ancerulus	oaiselon, ouuelet	auca	ouue, snayle
		auca iuuenis	saison
ancilla	baiselette	aucer	gars
ancillitas	baisselle	audit	ot
anelare	beer	auelana	noier
annus	an, anee	aures	oreilles
antequam	ancois, auant	auus	aiel, grant sire, le grant, monseigneur
aperire	ouurir		
apparare	apparailler, arraier, atirer		
approbare	esprouer	boviculus	boterel, petit buef
aptare	tailler		
aranca	eraine	bracce	brais, brais, les
ardea	herron	brachia	bras
aries	chastre,	brasium	brees

bufo	crepaude	conducit	louue
bullit	boelt	congregare	aerder, assembler
butirum	buire		
buxus	bochet	coquere	quir
caccare	chier	cor	cuer, le
caccauit	chioit	corulus	coure
cadere	cheoir, tresbucher	craticula	graille, vne
		crepare	creuer
calcaria	esporons	crines	chiueux
calidi	see cineres	cubiti	coutes
calige	chauces	culpare	afoler
campane	saintes	culpare	blamer, honir
canis	chien; mastyn, vn	culus	cuel
		cupa	cupe, vne
capella	chapel, vn	cuprum	cueure
capicium	chaperoun, vn	dealbare	blancher
capistrum	cheuestre, vn	dealbare	Buer
capra	cheure	decalciare	dechaucier
captiuus	chaitif, chiche, enfrim, trop tenant	decipere	trainer, tremeler
		deficit	faut
		deligare	delier, resoluer
caput	teste		
cauilla	cheuille	dentes	dens
cerebrum	ceruel, le	deponere	bouter, ouster, toller, tollir
cineres calidi	breis		
cingere	signer	deridere	escharnir, moker
cirotece	Gans		
cito	ades, yendrois	derisio	derision
claudere	fermer, clore	derisio	escharn, mokerie, mokeson
cocus	quisiner		
collum	col		
concordancia	accordance, accordement, accort	descendere	aualer, descendre
		deuiare	fforuoier, marrir

deuorare	deuorer, englouter, goulper, trans-glouter	factura	faceoun
		falsitas	fauxine
		fames	faim
		fauces	iouues
		fel	fiel, le
digiti	dois	ferrare	ferrer
diligere	amer	ferraui	ferrai
docere	apprendre, enseigner	fetare	vesser, vener
		fetens	puant
dolet	duelt	fetere	puir
domicella	damoisele, fillette	fetes	*see tu fetes*
		fetet	*see ille fetet*
dormis	dors	fetor	pui
dorsum	dos	fibule	noeaus
dubitare	douter, redoubter, sourcier	filiola	filiole, filluaille
		filiolus	filiol, filuoil
ducere	conuoier, demesner, mener	filum	fil, filet
		fimus	fiens
		findere	fendre
emendare	adubber, amender	finire	acheuer
		fiola	burette
epar	faye; foye, le	fissure	fendure
equales	egales, oueles	fistula	fretele, tiphielet; *see also parua fistula*
euellere	esracher, essartir, estirper		
exclamare	forscrier	flagellare	flaeller
expandere	espandre, estendre	fodere	fouir
		foramen	pertuz, treu
expectare	attendre	frangere	pecier
exstinguit	estaint	frangunt	pecient
extransuerso	a trauers	fraxinus	frasne
fac	fai	frenum	brinde, vne; frein, vn
faciam	ferai		

frons	front	incendium	brasier
fumosus	fumous	inferius	aual, deius
fumus	fume	inferre	combatre
fundare	founder	integra	enterine, entiere
fundit	founde		
gaudere	esbatre, sesbatre	iocus	esbatement, gale
genua	genoilles	iratus	corroucez, marri
grus	grue		
guttur	gorge, gorget	ire – vado	vais
hauriens	puisant	iunctae	iointes
haurire	puiser	iungere	ioindre
hauriunt	espuisent, puissent	labia	lieures
		lactare	alaitier
heresis	bougrenie, heresie	lancea	gleue, launce
		latrare	baier
hereticus	bougre, heretic	laudat	louue
		laus	loenge, los
herinacius	herison, heriz, oaie	lepararius	leuerer
		lepus	leuure
hirsutus	veluz	ligamina	liens, ligacions, ligatures, obligacions
hodie	hui		
homo	homme, len, on		
hora	leure		
hostium	huys	ligare	lier
iacere	coucher, giser	ligatus	liez
iactare	ietter, ruer	lignum	arbre, fust
iam	ja non	limax	lymache
ignis	see *paruus ignis*	lingua	langue
		liripipium	cornet, vn
ille fetet	puit	longitudo	longuesce, longure
in	ou		
incantator	enchantour, enfementer, erbuse	longum tempus	Guerres
		loqui	soner
		lucrare	gaigner

ludere	esbatre, sesbatre	natiuus	Neif
		nauis	Nief
lupus	lu	necesse	mestir
maior	greindre	nerui	nerfs, les
mamille	mamelles	nix	noif
— mulierum	tetes	nocere	annoier, nuyser
manere	maindre		
manus	mains	non	goute, graine, ja, ia rien, mye, nient, non, pas, point
mare	meer		
maritus	baroun, marit		
mater	miere		
matrina	marrine		
medicus	mire	nouem	noef
medulla	mouelle	nubes	nues
melius	miendre	nuces	noes
mentum	menton	nudus	nuz
meta	meute	nunquam	ja, non
meum dorsum	dors	nupcie	noces
miluus	estofle	obumbrare	enombrer
minus	menour	ocree	botes
mittere	enuoier, mander, tramettre	oculi	yeux
		oculis innuere	guinher
		oculus	oeil
monedula	kauue	odorabis	tu sentiras
mouere	bouger, moeuer	odorere	flairer
		odorere	odorer
multum	Guerres	operari	ouerir
munire	garnir	oportet	faut
mus	soriz	optare	regreter
musca	musche, vole	os	bouche
mutat	muet	ossa	os
mutus	mue	ouis matrix	oaille
nares	narins	palma	paume
nasci	naistre	palpabis	Tu sentiras
nasus	nies	palpebre	surcilz
natare	naire	parcere	esparnir

parebit	parra	pistor	bolengier,
parua fistula	flogot, fluhute		ffourner,
paruus ignis	fuet		patiser,
pascere	paistre		pestour
passer	moisson	pistrire	quir pestier
patella	paelle, vne		quir
pati	compasser,	planta mei	plane de mon
	deporter,	pedis	pie, la
	endurer,	pollex	posser
	souffrer	pompator	bobanceour,
patria	paijs		vantour
patrinus	parrin	ponderans	poisant
pauo	poun	pondus	pois
pauor	crainte,	potens	peus, puissant
	cremeur,	potestas	peu
	paour	premium	loier, merite
pax	paix	pronuba	makerellefe,
pecia rotunda	gobre, vn		makere-
pecten	penyl		umas
pectus	poitrine	proximi	prosmes,
pedens	peiant		voisins
pedere	peire	pugnare	combatre
pedes	pies	pulmo	pulmoun, le
pellis	pel, la	pulsare	soner
percuciam	fererai	pungere	poigner
percute	fer	radere	rere
percutere	ferir, fraper,	radius solis	raye
	torcher	ramunculi	ramsiaux
perforare	percer,	rana	raine
	pertuser	rapere	rauoier
perimplere …		raucus	arouue
equos	abuurer	recognoscere	confesser, re-
pica	agase		cognoistre,
pilius	pilioun, vn		regehir,
pisa	pois		vouer
pissa	pais	regulus	roitel

renes	reynes, les	spatule	espaules
reprobare	laidanger, reprendre, reprouer	speculari	mirer, mirer, remirer
		spernere	espernir
retia	las, reis	splen	splen, le
reumaticus	arumee	stomacus	stomac, le
riuoli	ruissiaux	stramen	estreim, paille
rotunda	see pecia rotunda	stultus	conort, fol, musart, sot
salix	sauche	stupefactus	abaiez
sancte	saintes	submersus	Noiez
sancti	sanis	sudare	suer
sanus	sanis	suere	coustre
scabellum	scelle	superbus	fumous
scabies	gale, roigne	supercilia	surcilles
scabiosus	galous, roignous	superius	amont, dessus
		tacere	coier, taiser
scalde, to	eschauder	talus	taloun
scalpere	grater	tarde et vix	Enuis
scies	Tu sentiras	temperies	temps
scindere	cier	temptare	assaier, attamer
scintilla	buette		
sedibitur	serrez	tempus	temps
separare	soiourer	tena	barette, vn
sequi	suir	tendere	tendre
serare	Sarrer	tergere	essuer, torcher
set	ains, mais	testiculi	coillons
si	Se	thretebolle	gorgat, le
sic	Si	tibie	iambes
siligo	sigle	timere	craindre, cremir
simia	cynge		
simulare et luere	comparer	timidus	crainant, cremeteus, paourous
situla	siel, vn		
soluere et dimittere	finer	tingere	taindre
sotulares	soliers	toga	hopelande, vne

tondere	tondre	vesica	vessie, la
tonges	tenelles	vespertilio	sorischau
trahere	sachier, tirer, traire	vigere	chiner
		vincere	conquerre, vaincre
tremere	tremeler		
tripes	troipie, vn	virescere	rauerder
tu fetes	pus	viscera	bodeyns; boiaux, les; boyaux; entrailles
turpis	lede, orde		
umbrare	ombrer		
vado	vais		
vaginare	gainer		
vbi	ou	vitrum	verre, vn
vel	ou	vix	see tarde et vix
vene	veynes	vmbelicus	vmbril
venter	ventre	vngues	vngles
vepres	rounces	vouere	vouer
verberare	batre	vrsus	ours
veretrum	vit	vulpes	guopil, regnart
vernus	ver		
vertere	verser	ymmo	ancois

Vernacular Words Used for Translation

adrad	c[ra]ins, cremuz, espoentez	debate, to	barater
		deius	aual
		deluere, a	faniour
aged	enuielly, enviesy	do, a	deyme
		doke, a	ane anet
ancle, an	cheuille	dokes mete	lentille
bake, to	pestier	dokes mete	viande des annes
beech	bochet		
belwe, a	sufflet, vn	drye your handes	essuez vox mains
bittir	amer		
blade of a knyf, a	lemele	dychere, a	ffosseour
body, the	corps, le	egge	trenchant
book, a	liure	ellir tre, an	sehu, vn
boste, to	bobancer, vanter	estanche, to	estancher
		fade, to	fluir
box	bochet	fadith	fleint
brestplate, a	peitryne	faren	*see* how faren ye
brewe hous, a	bracerie		
buke, a	deyn	fat, a	keuue, vne
buttokes	hanches	faxwax, the	vendon, le
calf, the	assure, le	fist, a	poign
calle, a	reiteal, vn	fleshhooke, a	crooke, vn
cart naue, a	moel	folde, to	plier
caste doun, to	abatre	forsake and go wood	forsener
cherl	villain		
chyken, a	poucyn	froward	rebours
clothes, the	draps, les	fryyngpanne, a	lechefryt, vn
cokerel, a	poulet	fulmard, a	martrir
cold	*see* it is gret cold	fyste	vesser, vener
		fyste, to	vesser
continuelment	ades	glade, to	hetier, rehetier
contrare, the	rebours	gloues of plate	gancellettes de feer
cowherde, a	vacher		
croper, a	culer, vn	goshauke, a	ostour
crowe, a	cornaille	grand dame	Beaulole
daubere, a	plasterer	gray	vair

grece	sain	kuttynge	trenchant
gret	see it is gret cold	laskes	flanks
		likerous	friande
gristel	tendroun	likerous	lechierres
groom, a	varleton	loke, to	sarrer
grownden	molu	loth	enuys
grype, to	empoigner	loue, to	amer
guttur	gorge, gorget	make fast, to	sarrer
hamme, the	garet de ma, iambe, le	marmuset	mimonet
		maser, a	madre, vn
hanselle	estreine	maugre my teeth	enuis
handes	mains		
hefre, a	joeuece	midryfe	marrite, le
hemp	chenure	mist	broilart, brouuez, browez
hen chyken, a	poule		
here thyng	leure		
hesil	coure	molle	mole
heuy	pesant	molten	fondu, oint, sain
hirid	lowez		
hoor	chanuz	mowere, a	facheour
horn, an	cornet	my knyf is rusty	Mon cotel est roillie
hors	chiual		
hous	see brewe hous	nosel, a	chardonet
housbonde, an	menager	now	ades, ia
how faren ye	coment faites vous	old	enviesy
		ouerthwerte	trauerser
howswyf, a	menagre	parmy	Aual
hynde, a	berche	paunce, a	pesse de mail
hyred	de lowage	pauor	crainte, cremeur, paour
iape	gas		
iapere, a	fateras		
it is gret cold	Il fait grant froit	pece, a	tasse dargent, vn
it is no iape	Il nest pas gas	penneknyf, a	trencheplume
kakele, to	kaqueter	penser	compasser
knede, to	pestier	pentys, a	Eiectice
knede, to	pestier	pilwer, a	orailler
knyf	cotel	pin, an	cheuille

plowman, a	charruer	stiropes	estruz
pouche, a	tassete	stool, a	scelle, vn
pound, a	liure	storke, a	cigoigne
pyn, a	chiuille	streynour, a	estamyn, vn
pynnes	espingles	stryke, a	raye
pynsouns	cafignouns	swan, a	cine
quisshyn, a	quarreau, vn	swynherde, a	porcher
rauene, a	corber	sydes	coustees
rigbon, the	eschyn, l'	syn þat tyme	puissedy
ruddoke, a	verder	taillour, a	cousturer
rusty	roillie	take me my	baillez moy mes
sawe, a	sye		
scherere, a	siour	pynsouns	cafignouns
score, a	taye	talwhe	sieu
score, a	taye	tame	priuee
score, to	taier	the body	le corps est
secree	priuee	is withynne	souz deinz
seem, a	cousture	the toumbe	lame
sharp	trenchant	the tree is old	larbre est
sherere, a	siour	or aged	enviesy
sheres	siselles	this	come len
shoure, to	Escurer	is a	pooit dire
slinge, a	founde	froward	cestui est
smeltes	espelankes	cherl	villain rebours
snake, a	noruez		
snyte your nose	mouchez vostre nies	this is an hyred hors	cest chiual de lowage
snyte, a	betar	thresshere, a	flaellour
soeffrer	compasser	thretebolle	gorget, le
sone	ades	thrusshe, a	mauys
sone	ia	thrustil cok, a	chardonet
sope	savon	thyghes	quysses
sowe, a	truye, vne	tikele, to	chatiller
sperhauke, a	esperuer	tipet, a	cornet
starlynge, a	estournel	titemose, a	mosenge
stepfadir	parastre	tonges	Molais
stepfmodir	marastre	tost	ades
		toumbe, the	lame

tree, the	arbre, l'	wrynge the clothes	tordez les draps
trestle, a	brichet, vn		
tubbe, a	cake, vn		
v. tre, an	hife	wrynge, to	tortir
vndo, to	anientiser, arierisser, deffaire	wrythe, to	tortir
		wype your eyen	terdez voz yeulx
walnote tre	noier	wype your handes	essuez vox mains; torchez voz mains
welke, to	flenir, fluir		
welkith	fleint		
wesil, a	fouma		
wet	moilee		
wexe reed, to	rouger	y am aged	Je suy envielly
what do ye	qe faites vous	y am loth	Je suy enuys
While he was there	tantdyz qil y feust	y cam for not elles	Je ne vyns pur el
whippe, a	fouet	y dide it maugre my teeth	Je le fiz enuis
whitrat, a	mustele		
wilw	sauche		
wortes	jontes	yolke, a	moeille

Index of Modern English Words Used as Glosses

a	22, 25–27, 31, 35, 39–41, 47–48, 58–65, 71, 77, 79	anus	55
		appear	37
		apple	56
		appropriately	42
		are	50
abdomen	71	armor	71
above	3	armpits	53
across	42	arms	21, 53
act	25	arrogant	46
Adams	56	arteries	58
adj.	3, 8–10, 12, 14–15, 17, 19–20, 29, 31–34, 36–37, 40, 44–49, 77	artistry	33
		as	77
		ash	75
		astray	12
		at	3, 5, 15–16, 33, 52
admit	9	attack	18
adv.	3, 5, 16, 29, 41–42, 45, 47, 50	attention	15, 33
		await	43
		away	16, 42, 47–48
adv./conj.	4, 44	back	23, 52, 54
affected	19	bake	38, 48
afraid	8	baker	6, 63
aged	78	bark	20
agreement	5	barley	74
all	16	barnacle-goose	71
along	44	bat	70
am	78	bawd	31
amazed	21	be	9, 12, 34, 45
ambiguous	44	bear	65
amuse	18	beat	18
amusement	13	before	4, 44
an	59, 76–77	befoul	41
and	10, 44–50, 76	bellows	63
angry	15	bells	48
ankle	23, 45, 56	belly	54

below	3		brewery	21
bench	61		bridle	64
bench-cover	61		bring	79
beneath	3, 44		buck	66
better	31		bucket	63
bind	31		building	27
bird	31, 70		bull	6
bitter	33, 45		burst	22
blackbird	69		but	4
bladder	58		butter	20
blade	53, 77		buttocks	55
blame	7		buttons	34
blood	58		by	19
bloodflow	24		cackle	29
blow	76		calf	55
blush	39		came	77
boast	21		cap	59
boat	33		cartilage	52
body	51, 56		cast	35
boils	20		cause	20
bonds	13		changes	33
bone	32		chatter	29
bones	54		cheeks	52
book	30		chest	53
boots	60		chicken	67
born	34		chin	52
bound	31		choler	58
bowels	57		chop	40
bowl	62		chough	69
boxwood	75		churl	77
braggart	17		clasp	24
brain	56		clean	49
brambles	39		cleanse	6
branches	38		clip	43
break	36, 38, 43		close	19
breastplate	71		close-fitting	59
breasts	54		clothes	24, 77
breeches	21, 59		clouds	34

coals	21	defecated	22
coat	59	delay	5
cold	50	delver	72
color	43	descend	4
compare	45	destroy	5
complete	23	devour	10
completely	44	diaphragm	57
confess	9	did	77
conj.	4, 40, 44, 50	difficulty	47
conj./adv.	*see adv./conj.*	dig	25
conquer	17	ditch-digger	72
continuously	45	do	26, 50
contrary	44	doe	66
cook	38, 48, 64	dog	65
copper	22	dogfish	75
country	37	dogs	20
coverings	61	doing	50
covers	71	door	29
cowherd	72	doublet	59–60
crack	27	doubt	10
crane	68	down	10, 13, 18, 27
creation	25	drag	39
criticize	14	drain	47
cross	42	draw	36, 38
crow	69	drawing	37
crupper	64	drinking	62
crushed	32	drowned	34
cry	22	dry	24, 76
cup	62	duck/duckling	68
currently	5	duckweed	15
cushion	61	dung	26
cutting	49	dye	43
dance	8	ears	51
darken	35	edge	49
day	78	egg	32
dead	10	elbows	53
deceive	42, 49	elder	76
defecate	22	else	77

embrace	20	fight	18
enchanter	12	fill	44
end	32	filthy	14
endure	9	fingers	53
entrails	6	finish	23
equals	35	fire	21, 27
equip	4	fist	24
erase	39	fit	25, 41
ermine	66	flanks	54
escort	15	fleshhook	63
esp.	71	flourish	22
establish	27	flute	12
etc.	62	fly	43, 67
ewe	65	fold	24
excite	22	follow	41, 44
expect	43	fool	10
extend	11	foolish	10
extinguishes	24	foot	56
eye	34	footwear	23
eyebrows	51	for	24, 45, 47, 77
eyelids	51	forehead	51
eyes	51, 76	forgive	46
fade	25	forsake	46
fades	47	foul	14
fall	10	found	27
falsehood	25	four	58
fart	17, 38, 43	fox	19
farting	38	fragrant	12
fashion	41	friend	4
fasten	39	frog	67
fastener	23	frying	62
fat	41	fur	44
fear	7–8, 10	gain	28
fearful	8	gall-bladder	57
feed	38	gauntlets	71
feet	56	give	31
felt	59	gladden	29
female	4, 48	glass	67

gloves	60	he	22–24, 27, 30, 33, 35–37, 57, 79
gluttonous	14		
go	12, 43, 46		
goat	25, 65	head	51, 61, 72
goblet	62	headdress	45, 60
goddaughter	13, 74	healthy	48
godfather	73	hears	35
godmother	73	heart	57
godson	13, 74	heavy	37
goose	35, 68, 71	hedgehog	66
goshawk	70	heel	56
gosling	68	heifer	64
grandfather	74	helmet	71
grandmother	20, 74	hemp	25
grasses	29	hen	67
gray	40, 44	herbs	29
grease	41	Here	44
greased	34	heresy	7
great	59	heretic	7
greater	29	heron	68
greedy	9	hind	66
green	39	hires	30
greyhound	30	hit	19, 26–27
grill	63	hoarse	20
grip	24	hole	16
groin	55	homeland	37
ground	32	hood	58–59
hair	24, 51	horn	45
hairnet	60–61	horse	25–26, 79
hairpins	61	horses	44
hairy	44	hose	60
halter	64	hostile	77
hamstring	55	hot	21
hands	53, 76	hour	30
hare	30	household	72
harm	5, 16	housewife	72
hat	59	How	50
hazel	75	hub	31

human	51	lark	31, 69
humours	58	larynx	56
hunger	26	lead	15
husband	15	learn	44
I	26, 36, 77–78	lecherous	14
if	40	legs	55
immediately	3, 29, 45	length	15
implore	28	lentil	15
in	50	lesser	31
injure	16	lie	13, 25
insane	46	limit	32
instrument	12	line	39
intact	12	lips	30, 52
interior	56	liripipe	59
into	41	little	27
iron	25	liver	26, 57
is	28–29, 46, 50, 76–79	lock	39, 48
		long	47
it	20, 46–47, 76–77	look	15, 33
		love	33, 45
jackdaw	69	lover	4
jerkin	59	lung	57
join	29	magpie	69
joints	53	maidservant	21–22, 73
joke	13, 76	make	26
kerchiefs	61	male	48, 73
kidneys	57	malt	74
kindle	21	man	15, 35
kite	70	mantle	60
knead	38, 48	maple	62
knees	55	mark	39, 48
knife	77–78	marriage	34
know	49	marrow	32
lacking	46	marten	66
lady	13	mastiff	65
ladybird	71	me	79
lady-in-waiting	13	melancholy	58
lance	71	melted	34

melts	27	nostrils	52
mend	3	not	16
might	77	note	34, 40–41, 46, 78
milk	31		
mist	6, 21	nothing	77
mittens	60	now	47
mock	11	noxious	46
mockery	11	*num.*	33
monkey	65–66	nuts	33
mother	32	of	20, 25, 27, 31, 48, 51–52, 56, 60, 72, 77
mouse	40		
mouth	52		
move	6	off	23
mower	41, 73	old	78
much	47	omen	24
mute	32	on	44
my	51–56, 78–79	one	77
		oneself	11, 18
n.	3–17, 19–27, 29–41, 43–45, 48–49, 58, 60–61, 63–77	open	35
		opposite	77
		or	9–12, 24, 30, 39, 49–50, 57, 59, 62, 67, 78
nails	53	out	11, 22
naked	34	outer	59
names	51	pair	60
nasal	52	palm	53
natural	33	paltock	60
navel	54	pan	62
necessary	46	part	27, 37–38
necessity	33	parts	51
neck	52	pay	15, 33
neighbors	16	payment	14
nerves/tendons	58	peace	37
never	29, 47	peacock	70
nine	33	peas	37
no	76	peg	23
nose	51, 76	penis	54

penknife	72	present	5
perspire	41	prick	24
phlegm	58	procurer/procuress	31
physician	33	projecting	27
pierce	16, 24	prove	23
pike	75	provide	47
pillow	35	pubes	55
pin	45	pull	19, 39
pins	24	pullet	67
pipe	12	punished	45
pitch	37	pure	12
pitcher	20	purse	58
pl.	13–14, 16, 21, 24, 29–30, 33–35, 37–39, 41, 48, 58, 60–61, 63–64, 71	quilted	60
		ram	65
		rape	39
		raven	69
		ray	48
		reach	43
		reaper	41, 73
plasterer	73	recognize	50
play	18, 45	recorder	12
pleasure	45	redden	39
plowman	72	*rel. pron.*	50
polecat	66	release	46
polish	40	remain	31
poss. pron.	30	remove	16, 42
pot	20	rented	31, 79
potent	36	rents	30
pound	30	reproach	14
pours	27	resemble	18
power	36	reverse	43
powerful	36–37	reward	14
pr.	50	robin	70
praise	14, 30	rubbish	26
praises	30	rusty	78
prep.	3, 42, 44, 50	rye	74
prepare	4	saints	48
pres.	37–38	saw	40

say	48, 77	silent	9
scab	19, 39	silver	62
scabby	19	since	78
scabies	19	skin	58
scald	25	sleep	23
scissors	41	sling	27
scorn	23	slippers	79
scour	40	slowly	47
scrape	39	small	12, 58, 66, 70
scratch	28	small-worm	67
sea	32	smell	12, 49
seam	22	smelt	74
season	44	smoke	26
seat	62	snail	67
secret	47	snake	67
see	34, 40–41, 46, 78	snares	14
		snipe	70
seize	39	snow	33
send	17	so	41
servant	73	soap	41
sew	22	soft	32
shade	35	soil	41
shadow	35	sole	56
sharp	3, 49	some	17
sharpen	5	something	11
shatter	36, 38	soon	29
shear	43	sound	48
shears	41	sow	64
sheathe	28	spare	23
ship	33	spark	20
shirt	59	sparrow	69
shod	26	spearhawk	23, 70
shoe	25	spider	67
shoes	60	spine	54
shoulder	53	spleen	57
shoulders	52	split	27
shut	19	spread	11
sides	54	spring	44

spurs	60	tame	47
starling	69	tapestry	61
staunch	24	tar	37
stay	5	teach	4, 44
steer	6	tear	11
stepfather	73	teeth	52
stepmother	73	tendon	52
stink	36, 38	test	4
stinking	38	testicles	55
stinks	36	that	28–29, 71, 76, 78
stirrups	64		
stomach	57	the	44, 48, 51–52, 54–59, 77–78
stool	40, 62		
stop	24		
stork	70	their	30
strainer	63	there	79
straw	11	they	36
streams	39	thighs	55
stretch	43	think	45
strike	18–19, 42, 49	this	77, 79
stripe	39, 48	thread	13
suckle	31	three-legged	62–63
suet	41	thresher	72
suffer	9, 45	throat	13, 52
suffers	23	throw	18
suitably	42	thrush	69
sun	48	thumb	37
surly	77	thus	41
swallow	10	thwart	42
swan	68	tickle	22
sweat	41	time	47, 49
swim	34	tippett	45
swineherd	72	tit	70
table	61	to	3–25, 27–29, 31, 33–35, 38–50
tailor	22		
take	16, 23, 42, 45		
tallow	41	toad	67
tally	48	today	29

toes	56	weighing	37
tongs	63	weight	37
tongue	52	wet	32
too	76	what	50
touch	43, 49	wheel	31
traps	14	where	50
tree	75–76, 78	while	79
tremble	49	whip	25, 27
trickster	26	whistle	12
tripod	63	white-haired	40
trivet	63	whiten	6
trouble	20	whole	12
tub	63	will	26, 37, 49
tunic	59	willow	75
turn	39, 43	wind	43
twist	42	wink	28
twist/bend	49	wipe	49, 76
twist/squeeze	49	with	25, 39, 47
unbind	11	wither	25
unfortunate	9	withers	47
unruly	77	wolf	30, 65
unwilling	78	womb	54
unwillingly	77	women's	54
upper	53	wood	12, 27, 40, 62
uproot	11	words	44
vat	63	work	35
veins	58	wren	70
very	50	wring	42, 77
vetch	74	yarn	13
vow	50	year	3
wait	5	yew	75
walnut	76	yolk	32
was	79	you	23, 26–27, 36, 49–50
water	15, 36–38, 44	young	6, 13, 22, 67–68
watery	20	your	76
weapon	27		
weasel	66		
weather	49		

Dictionary Headwords Cited in the Notes to the Edition[2]

ABELLANA (DMLBS)	76	aval (AND)	44
abreuver (DMF)	44	aval (AND)	44
abreuveur (DMF)	44	avouer (AND)	50
aduber (AND)	3	AXILLA (DMLBS)	53
affiler (DMF)	5	baer (AND)	21
affoler (DMF)	7	baisaux (AND)	22
afiler (AND)	5	baisselle (DMF)	22
afoler (AND)	7	beer (Godefroy)	21
aine (AND)	55	beer (OFrD)	21
ainz (AND)	4	bekas (AND)	70
aler (AND)	43	belole (DMF)	20
ANCERULUS (Du Cange)	68	*bernak(e* (MED)	71
ANCILLATUS (DMLBS)	22	biche (AND)	66
ane (AND)	55	bisse (AND)	66
ANELARE (DMLBS)	21	blaret (AND)	71
anete (AND)	68	blason (AND)	53
ANSERCULUS (DMLBS)	68	bobance (AND)	17
apentiz (AND)	27	bobancer (DMF)	21
appentis (DMF)	27	bobanceur (DMF)	17
arouer (AND)	20	bochet (AND)	75
arterie (MED)	58	bougrenie (OFrD)	7
asperner (DMF)	23	bouvelet (DMF)	6
atamer (DMF)	4	bovicle (AND)	6
atendre (AND)	43	BRACIUM (DMLBS)	74
attamen (MED)	4	braie (AND)	21
atteignaument (AND)	42	brais (AND)	74
atteindre (AND)	42	brochet (DMF)	75
atteindre (AND)	43	brochete (AND)	75
ATTINGERE (DMLBS)	42	broil (AND)	6
ATTINGERE (DMLBS)	43	brouillard (DMF)	6
AUDIRE (DMLBS)	35	broume (AND)	6

---

2) In this index, French words are presented in roman, English in italic and Latin in small capitals. The relevant dictionary follows the entry and is given in parenthesis.

buer (AND)	6	CONVENIENTER (DMLBS)	42
buer (DMF)	6	cordellot. (AND)	61
buette (DMF)	20	cornard (DMF)	10
bugerie (AND)	7	cornart (AND)	10
buillir (AND)	20	corucer (AND)	15
buis (AND)	75	CORYLUS (DMLBS)	75
BULGARUS (DMLBS)	7	coudre (AND)	75
BULLIRE (DMLBS)	20	couvrechyefs. (AND)	61
CALIGA (DMLBS)	79	criendre (AND)	7
caliges (Cotgrave)	79	croller (AND)	8
calle (MED)	60	crouler (DMF)	8
CAPTIVARE (Du Cange)	9	cuire (AND)	38
caqueter (DMF)	29	cuivre1. (AND)	22
caroler (AND)	8	CUPA (DMLBS)	62
caroller (DMF)	22	cuppe (AND)	62
ceindre (AND)	40	*cuttinge* (MED)	49
chardon (AND)	69	*dauber* (MED)	73
chardonnet (DMF)	69	deim (AND)	66
chastri (DMF)	65	deime (AND)	66
chatoiller (AND)	22	dejus (AND)	3, 44
chatouiller (DMF)	22	*delver* (MED)	72
chatri (AND)	65	DEPONERE (DMLBS)	16
chaufsoris (AND)	70	*dicher* (MED)	72
choue (AND)	69	DIMITTERE (DMLBS)	46
cimer (DMF)	22	DOLORE (DMLBS)	23
CINGERE (DMLBS)	40	dormir (AND)	23
coi (AND)	9	DORMIRE (DMLBS)	23
coi (MED)	9	doseur (DMF)	61
coillart (AND)	65	dossiere (DMF)	61
compassant (AND)	9	douloir (AND)	23
COMPASSARE (DMLBS)	9	*eller* (MED)	76
COMPASSATIO (DMLBS)	9	embatre (AND)	18
compasser (AND)	9	embattre (DMF)	18
COMPASSIO (DMLBS)	9	enbeverer (AND)	44
compassion (AND)	9	enchantur (AND)	12
COMPASSUS (DMLBS)	9	endreit (AND)	3
CONDUCERE. (DMLBS)	30	enfrener (AND, DMF)	9
continuelment (AND)	45	enombrer (DMF)	35

entamen (MED)	4	*fax-wax* (MED)	52
entamer (AND)	4	feie (AND)	26
enumbrer (AND)	35	feindre (AND)	25
enviellir (AND)	78	feindre (AND)	47
enviezir (AND)	78	ferir (AND)	26–27
envis (Cotgrave, DMF)	78	FERRARE (DMLBS)	26
enviz (AND)	47, 78	ferrer (AND)	26
epa (MED)	57	FETARE (DMLBS)	17
epar (MED)	26	FETERE (DMLBS)	36
épingle (DMF)	24, 61	fien (AND)	26
épuiser (DMF)	36	fiens (DMF)	26
esbahir (AND)	21	FIMUM (DMLBS)	26
esbatre (AND)	45	finer (AND)	46
eschine (AND)	54	*fissure* (MED)	27
escufle (AND)	70	*fist* (MED)	17
espinel (AND)	61	flaeler (AND)	72
espuiser (AND)	36	flaeller (DMF)	72
essele (AND)	53	flaelur (AND)	72
estaindre (AND)	24	flageller (TLF)	72
estamine (AND)	63	flaistrer (AND)	25
estreim (AND)	24	flammir (DMF)	25
estrepe (AND)	11	flanc (AND)	54
estriu (AND)	64	flétrir (DMF)	25
étamine (DMF)	63	fluer (AND)	47
eu (MED)	75	fluir (DMF)	47
EXSTINGUERE (DMLBS)	24	FOETOR (DMLBS)	36
extirper (DMF)	11	fosseur (AND, DMF)	72
FACERE (DMLBS)	26	FRANGERE (DMLBS)	36
façun (AND)	25	friande (AND)	14
faden (MED)	47	friandise (OFrD)	14
faillir (AND)	46	friand-lecheur (DMF)	14
faire (AND)	26	*fulmard* (MED)	66
faire (AND)	50	fumeux (DMF, FEW)	46
faneur (DMF)	72	FUMOSUS (DMLBS)	46
fast(e (MED)	48	fumous (AND)	46
fastras (TL)	26	funder (AND)	27
fateras (AND)	26	FUNDERE (DMLBS)	27
fatras (DMF)	26	fundre (AND)	27

fwyne (AND)	66	INCANTATOR (DMLBS)	12
gab (AND)	76	INFERRE (DMLBS)	18
gaine (AND)	28	*–ise* (MED)	27
galeux (DMF)	19	ja (AND)	29
galle (Cotgrave, DMF)	19	joe (AND)	52
galle (MED)	19	jonc (DMF)	29
galleux (Cotgrave)	19	junc (AND)	29
gant (AND)	71	jupon (AND)	59
gantelet (DMF)	71	juvence (AND)	64
gargate (DMF)	56	kölpos (FEW)	10
garnir (AND)	47	lace (AND)	14
GAUDERE, (DMLBS)	45	lame (DMF)	78
gerner (AND)	47	LAUDARE (DMLBS)	30
gole (TL)	10	lecher (AND)	14
gorgite (AND)	56	lechur (DMF)	14
graignur (AND)	29	lentille (AND)	15
grei (MED)	44	*leske* (MED)	54
grinden (MED)	32	limace (AND, DMF)	67
guenyler (AND)	28	limaçon (AND)	67
gueres (AND)	16	LIMAX (DMLBS)	67
gueres (AND)	47	loer (AND)	30
gueule (DMF)	10	loer (AND)	30
guigner (DMF)	28	LUCRARI (DMLBS)	28
gule (AND)	10	madre (DMF)	62
gulpen (MED)	10	maheutre (DMF)	53
gute (AND)	16	mahustre (AND)	53
guttur (MED)	13	maimonnet (DMF)	66
HAERESIS (DMLBS)	7	mainmonnet (Godefroy)	66
hanselle (MED)	24	marmeset (AND)	66
HAURIRE (DMLBS)	36	*marmusset* (MED)	66
HAURIRE (DMLBS)	36	marrene (AND)	73
HEPAR (DMLBS)	26	marrir (AND, DMF)	12
hif (AND)	75	martre (AND)	66
hiren (MED)	31	MATRINUS (DMLBS)	73
home (AND)	35	mauviz (AND)	69
housbonde (MED)	72	mazer (AND)	62
hous-wif (MED)	72	mes (AND)	4
iapere (MED)	26	mesnager (AND)	72

mesnere (AND)	72	orver (Cotgrave)	67
mester (AND)	33	orvet (DMF, TLF)	67
META (DMLBS)	32	*osel(e* (MED)	69
mete (AND)	32	overthwerten (MED)	42
meule (AND)	32	ovrer (AND)	35
mid-rif (MED)	57	owe (AND)	68
moel (DMF)	31	paistre (AND)	38
mol (AND)	32	palevole (AND)	43, 71
mol (MED)	32	pareir (AND)	37
mol (MED)	32	PARERE (DMLBS)	37
molet (DMF)	63	parmi (AND)	44
MOLLE (Du Cange)	32	PASCERE (DMLBS)	38
MOLLEX (DMLBS)	32	pâtissier (DMF)	6
MOLLIS (DMLBS)	32	*paunc* (MED)	71
mou (DMF)	32	*pece* (MED)	62
moudre, (AND)	32	peçoier (AND)	36
mous (MED)	40	PECTEN (DMLBS)	55
mouton (DMF)	65	peis (AND)	37
mucher (AND)	76	peisant (AND)	37
muel (AND)	31	peitrine (AND)	71
muer (AND)	33	penil (AND)	55
MUNIRE (DMLBS)	47	penser (AND)	45
MUSCA (DMLBS)	43	pentis (AND)	27
mustele (AND)	66	*pentis* (MED)	27
MUTARE (DMLBS)	33	PERCUTERE (DMLBS)	26–27
mutun (AND)	65	pes (AND)	36
naif (AND)	33	pester (AND)	38
neer (AND)	34	pinçun (AND)	79
neif (AND)	33	*pinson* (MED)	79
nerf (AND)	58	PISTARE (DMLBS)	38
nerve (MED)	58	piz (AND)	71
NON (DMLBS)	29	plastrer (AND)	73
oie (DMF)	68	poer (AND)	36
oindre (DMF)	34	poindre (AND)	24
oir (AND)	35	pois (AND)	37
oiselon (AND)	68	poitrine (DMF)	71
oison (DMF)	68	POSSE (DMLBS)	36
OPTARE (DMLBS)	28	privé (AND)	47

PRONUBA (DMLBS)	31	seimer (AND)	34
puir (AND)	36	sein (AND)	48
puiscedi (AND)	78	seint (AND)	48
puisier (AND)	36	séjourner (DMF)	40
rai (AND)	48	sentir (AND)	49
raimsel (AND)	38	SEPARARE (DMLBS)	40
RAMUNCULUS (DMLBS)	38	SERARE (DMLBS)	41
rate (AND)	57	SERRARE (DMLBS)	41
rebours (DMF)	77	serrer (AND)	41, 48
reburs (AND)	77	seu (AND)	76
RECOGNOSCERE (DMLBS)	50	seü (DMF)	76
regreter (AND)	28	severer (AND)	40
regretter (DMF)	28	*sherer(e* (MED)	41
rei (AND)	60	si (AND)	40, 41
rere (AND)	39	SI (DMLBS)	40
resolver (DMF)	11	SIC (DMLBS)	41
rete (DMF)	60	sier (AND)	40
RETICULUM (DMLBS)	60–61	sifflet (DMF)	12
reume (AND)	20	SIGNARE (DMLBS)	40
rhume (DMF)	20	signer (AND)	40
RIVOLUS (DMLBS)	39	sior (AND)	41
roigne (AND)	19	SITULA (DMLBS)	63
roigne (DMF)	19	*snail* (MED)	68
rougir (DMF)	39	SOJORNARE (DMLBS)	40
roujoier (AND)	39	SOLVERE (DMLBS)	46
ruddok(e (MED)	70	soucier (AND)	10
ruil (AND)	78	SPERARE (DMLBS)	40
russel (AND)	39	STIRPARE (DMLBS)	11
saker (AND)	39	*strepen* (MED)	11
sauce (DMF)	75	*strike* (MED)	48
sauz (AND)	75	SUBMERGERE (DMLBS)	34
scelle (AND)	62	suffrir (AND)	45
SCIRE (DMLBS)	49	suial (DMF)	68
score (MED)	48	sujurer (AND)	40
scouren (MED)	40	surcil (AND)	51
SEDERE (DMLBS)	41	surciller. (AND)	51
seer (AND)	41	suriz (AND)	70
seil (AND)	63	teindre (AND)	43

tenail (AND)	63	TRIPES (DMLBS)	63
TENDERE (DMLBS)	43	uel (AND)	35
tendre (AND)	43	*undon* (MED)	5
tete (AND)	54	VADERE (DMLBS)	43
tette (DMF)	54	vair (AND)	44
threshen (MED)	72	vent (AND)	17
thresher (MED)	72	venter (DMF, TLF)	17
throstel-cok (MED)	69	vereder (AND)	70
throte-bolle (MED)	56	vervis (AND)	65
tikelen (MED)	22	*vesic(e* (MED)	58
time (MED)	78	vessir (AND)	17
torcher (AND)	42	vessir (DMF)	43
tortir (DMF)	49	vol (AND, DMF)	43
tortre (AND)	42	vouer (AND, DMF)	50
tost (AND)	45	waynter (AND)	28
trahir (AND)	42	*welken* (MED)	47
traine (AND)	42	*wesel(e* (MED)	66
trainer (AND)	42	*whit-rat* (MED)	66
TRANSVERSUS (DMLBS)	42	*wort* (MED)	29
trembler (AND)	49	*wringen* (MED)	49
tremeler (DMF)	49	*writhen* (MED)	49
trencher (AND)	49		

www.ingramcontent.com/pod-product-compliance
Lightning Source LLC
Chambersburg PA
CBHW020837020526
44114CB00040B/1229